CHARLES JEN[

THE MAN BEHIND
HANDEL'S *MESSIAH*

CHARLES JENNENS

THE MAN BEHIND
HANDEL'S *MESSIAH*

Ruth Smith

HANDEL HOUSE TRUST
THE GERALD COKE HANDEL FOUNDATION

ACKNOWLEDGEMENTS

The author gratefully acknowledges the advice and assistance of Professor Donald Burrows, Open University; C. W. Hind FSA, Chief Curator and H.J. Heinz Curator of Drawings, RIBA British Architectural Library; Christopher Purvis CBE, President, Handel House Museum; Professor John H. Roberts, University of California, Berkeley; Anna Sander, Lonsdale Curator of Archives & Manuscripts, Balliol College, Oxford; Dr Mike Smith; Oliver Soden; Professor Colin Timms, University of Birmingham.

Front cover and frontispiece: Jennens by the premier portraitist of the mid 18th century, Thomas Hudson. This painting is undated but seems to be from the same period as the other Hudson portrait of Jennens (p. 2), the mid 1740s. Jennens also commissioned from Hudson the majestic and magnificently framed 'Gopsall' portrait of Handel (p. 48).
Back cover: Gopsall Hall as constructed by Jennens. This view, painted by an unknown artist some time after 1764, shows, at left, Jennens' monument to his friend Edward Holdsworth, crowned by the statue of Religion commissioned from Louis-François Roubiliac.

First co-published in the United Kingdom in 2012 by
Handel House Trust Ltd
25 Brook Street
London WIK 4HB
and
The Gerald Coke Handel Foundation
40 Brunswick Square
London WCIN IAZ

© 2012

ISBN 978-0-9560998-2-2

British Library Cataloguing-in-Publication Data

A Catalogue record for this book is available
from The British Library

Designed in Adobe Caslon by
Geoff Green Book Design, Cambridge CB24 4RA
Printed and bound by Gutenberg, Malta

CONTENTS

'Your Messiah'

FOREWORD

ITHOUT CHARLES JENNENS (1700–1773) we
would not have *Messiah*. Writing to Jennens from
Dublin in 1741, Handel called the libretto 'your oratorio
Messiah'. *Messiah* seems to have been Jennens' idea, and he
compiled the text on his own initiative. Jennens was Handel's
best English librettist, providing in addition to *Messiah* (1742)
the texts of *Saul* (1739), *Belshazzar* (1744), and probably *Israel
in Egypt* (1739), and writing *Il Moderato* for *L'Allegro, Il
Penseroso ed Il Moderato* (1740). All his librettos prompted
Handel to advance the development of oratorio.

Creating librettos for Handel was only part of Jennens'
achievements. A generous friend of the composer, to whose
music he was (by his own account) addicted, Jennens assembled the most comprehensive contemporary collection of his
works, in both manuscript and print. The Aylesford Collection,
named after Jennens' cousin to whom he bequeathed it,
contained in addition a wealth of Italian music. Though
dispersed by auctions in 1873 and 1918, its riches have been
largely identified by Handel scholars and constitute a vital
resource for Handel studies.

Jennens was moreover a great landowner; the creator of a
remarkable country house with extensive grounds; a major art
collector; a Christian philanthropist; a devout defender of
revealed religion; a scholarly encourager of other authors; a
loyal friend; and a pioneering editor of Shakespeare. The
jealous enmity aroused by this last endeavour, his position as a
political outsider, and his shy, depressive, irascible tempera-
ment, led to the eclipse of his reputation for nearly two
centuries. This book uncovers the outlines of his life, his
personality, and his achievements.

Jennens in his sixties; a characteristically delicate and detailed chalk drawing by Giles Hussey, an artist from Dorset who spent his early twenties employed by the British community in exile in Rome, where he produced a famous portrait of the Young Pretender (Bonnie Prince Charlie). There he probably also met Jennens' friend Edward Holdsworth, a Jacobite agent. Following his return to England, Hussey continued to attract the patronage of Catholics, Jacobites, and ideological Jacobites such as Jennens. Jennens may have been additionally interested in Hussey's theories of an alignment of proportion, musical notes and colours.

1

'I was born & bred in Leicestershire mud'

THE GENTLEMAN SCHOLAR

Opposite: Jennens portrayed by Thomas Hudson in 1747, when he became squire of Gopsall; a music score open behind him indicates his chief interest.

Overleaf: Below left: Erdington Hall, the Jennens' country residence in the 17th century. *Below right:* The original Gopsall Hall, where Jennens was born in 1700. *Above:* Gopsall Hall transformed: the mansion created by Jennens. This image of the south front was published by John Woolfe and James Gandon in 1767 in *Vitruvius Britannicus,* a sumptuous architectural survey of notable English Palladian houses. The relief of ships near a harbour in stormy weather was inscribed 'fortiter occupa portam' (Horace Odes 1:14), which could have a double political meaning – seek the shelter of the port, or, strongly seize the port.

JENNENS' DEPRECATING phrase about his upbringing, in a letter of 5 December 1743 to his close friend Edward Holdsworth, disguises origins about which he may have been self-conscious. His family had been Leicestershire landed gentry for only two generations. Gopsall Hall and its estate, his birthplace and lifelong home, had been bought by his grandfather in 1685, and his father was the first member of the family to live there. The family's previous country residence was Erdington Hall, in Warwickshire, only five miles away from the source of their prosperity. The immense Jennens wealth came from iron manufacture and the rise of Birmingham as Britain's industrial centre. Their Birmingham town house was considered the finest in the city, and a Jennens Road commemorates their many local benefactions. Already prominent in iron manufacture in the sixteenth century, by the end of the seventeenth century they were producing over 2000 tons of cast iron a year, and steadily buying up land, initially for wood to feed their furnaces and later for investment. By the end of the eighteenth century their land was valued at the modern equivalent of about £55 million, and when Jennens' father died in 1747 Jennens inherited thirty-four properties scattered over six counties as well as the 736 acres of Gopsall.

By the time Jennens was born the family was firmly related

to the established and cultivated landed gentry. Jennens' maternal grandfather, Sir Robert Burdett, was a Member of Parliament, as was Sir Robert's grandson and namesake, who was one of Jennens' executors. Jennens' aunt Jane Burdett married Sir John Cotton, grandson and namesake of the donor to the nation of the family's famous Cottonian manuscripts collection which formed the basis of the British Library; Jennens' letters show him to be in regular contact with this part of the family. Another uncle was Gentleman of the Bedchamber to King William III, and had a son to whom the king stood godfather: William Jennens of Acton, 'the miser', whose contested inheritance reputedly prompted the Jarndyce v

Jarndyce case in Dickens' *Bleak House*. Jennens was on particularly close terms with the family of yet another much-respected uncle, Sir Clement Fisher, whose daughter married the second earl of Aylesford. Jennens' sister Elizabeth was sought in marriage by William Lygon, heir of Madresfield, Worcestershire, but instead married her cousin William Hanmer, whose anciently established family had estates in Suffolk and Flintshire. Jennens was accustomed to, and welcome in, the grandest company. He was on equal terms with the aristocrats among the 'Brother Handelists', and his letters mention in passing that he has been staying as a guest at Burleigh and Chatsworth – unplanned visits in response to

Jennens' substantial London townhouse on the north side of Great Ormond Street, Bloomsbury, the scene of the dinner described in George Harris' diary for 29 May 1756 (p. 46) after which Handel played Jennens' piano. In the 19th century the adjoining Children's Hospital took over this house, which was demolished when the hospital was rebuilt.

impromptu invitations, which he plainly took in his stride.

The man who described himself as 'born & bred in Leicestershire mud' habitually spent the season in London. From 1729 to 1734 he paid rates on a house in Queen Square, Bloomsbury; for some years thereafter he shared the house of his brother-in-law William Hanmer, also in Queen Square. Hanmer worked in ecclesiastical administration in Middle Temple, and his clerk there, John Hetherington, who served as factotum in the Hanmer home as well, witnessed codicils to Handel's will – a connection that could have come through Jennens. From 1752 Jennens owned a handsome house round the corner in Great Ormond Street, on the site of the present entrance to the Hospital for Children.

Unlike his father, who had studied at Middle Temple and

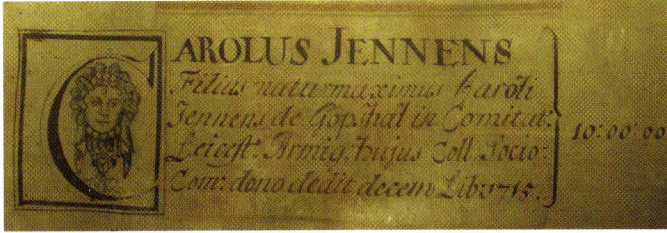

Balliol College Benefactors' Book 1684–1783, showing payment in December 1715 of £10, the usual fee, for Jennens' admission as a fellow-commoner. Each name on the page has a decorative initial letter. The pages of the book were originally posted up in college; pin holes are still visible in the corners.

became the local magistrate, Jennens entered Balliol College, Oxford, as a fellow-commoner, at the age of fifteen. Balliol was a popular choice among West Midlands gentry. Fellow-commoners, of whom over seventy were admitted between 1701 and 1717, were fee-paying, usually members of the upper gentry or minor aristocracy, and were excused the manual duties of scholars, but they were expected to fulfil the normal syllabus of tutorials and debates. A well-rounded education was available. Besides the traditional Oxford diet of classical literature, divinity, ethics and logic, Balliol could offer poetry, rhetoric, mathematics (pure and applied), Hebrew, geography, astronomy, modern history, biography and natural philosophy (sciences). Additional subjects such as modern languages could be studied with external tutors. Jennens' tutor was the recently appointed Joseph Sanford (Fellow 1714–74), only nine years older than Jennens and an example of erudition and of helpfulness to other scholars. There may be an indication of Jennens' already having developed an enthusiasm for music in the minutes of the Oxford Music Club: a Mr Jennings (the contemporary pronunciation of the name, and the one Jennens used) is listed as a paid-up non-performing member in January 1718, after three months on the waiting list.

Like most fellow-commoners (and maybe also on political grounds, see chapter 2) Jennens did not take a degree, but he stayed at Oxford long enough to acquire a thorough knowledge of Latin and Greek (evident in his epigraphs to *Saul* and his correspondence with Holdsworth), probably also some Hebrew (from Sanford), some close friendships, and a lifelong devotion to scholarship and to book collecting (shared with Sanford).

Jennens amassed an outstanding collection of early printings of Shakespeare's plays, which formed the basis for his groundbreaking editions of individual plays. The collection was auctioned in 1907 by Jennens' descendant, the 4th Earl Howe. The front page of the auction catalogue advertises the 'good' and rare second quarto (Q2) of *Hamlet* (1604/5), which with the first folio (of which Jennens also owned a copy) is the source text of modern editions.

First and Early Quarto Plays of William Shakespeare,

all bound in modern half blue morocco.

*** *Lots 1 to 28 will be first offered together as a Collection, but if the reserve price be not realised they will immediately afterwards be sold separately.*

Lot 1.

HAMLET. The/ Tragicall Historie of/ Hamlet,/ Prince of Denmarke./ By William Shakespeare./ Newly imprinted and enlarged to almost as much/ againe as it was, according to the true and Perfect/ Coppie./ *Contains* 51 *ll. including title*; *signs.* B-O 2 *the last leaf misprinted* G 2 ; *title stained and written on, some lower margins stained and a few catchwords and signatures cut into, lower plain outside corners of* I-K 2 *mended but not injuring the text* ; *text more or less injured in all the lower outside corners of* K 3 *to end, of which the words missing are supplied in MS. otherwise sound, clean and genuine throughout, measuring* 7 *by* 5 *in.*   sm. 4to
At London/ Printed by J. R. for N. L. and are to be Sold at his/ Shoppe under Saint Dunstons Church in/ Fleet Street, 1604
*** The Second Quarto Edition of Shakespeare's Hamlet, of which only three copies, including this one, are known. Lowdnes mentions all three, and no other copy

His loyalty to Balliol and to the wider University is evident in some of his book subscriptions. He was a passionate bibliophile. 'I, who buy all books …' he wrote in later life. The library he built up at Gopsall contained around 10,000 volumes, over 700 of them on theological topics. Already in his early twenties he subscribed to Alexander Pope's edition of Shakespeare, and he went on to compile an outstanding collection of the earliest printings of Shakespeare, including each of the first four folios and twenty-eight of the quarto texts preceding them.

Oxford and, perhaps, his devout Protestantism gave Jennens immense respect for verbal truth. Accuracy; honest representation and weighing of evidence; clear delivery of a worthwhile message – these were principles of paramount importance to him. They were evident in the last of his many acts of combined scholarship and encouragement of the arts. In his seventies, with splendid disregard for mortality, he made his Shakespeare collection the basis for a projected complete edition. He lived to finish five volumes: *King Lear* (1770), *Macbeth*, *Hamlet* and *Othello* (1773), and *Julius Caesar* (published posthumously in 1774). Although they are not in the front rank of informed or insightful interpretation, they are now regarded as more scholarly than any that preceded them: the first editions of Shakespeare texts to approach modern standards in textual criticism.

Jennens planned to issue each play as a separate volume, a commonplace of modern publishing which was then unprecedented. He surpassed his predecessors in care and precision, citing and acknowledging both texts and previous editors in more scrupulous detail than was customary. His notes repeatedly convey appreciation of Shakespeare's style and of the drama in

The last known portrait of Jennens, by Mason Chamberlin the elder, a founding member of the Royal Academy and a pupil of Francis Hayman, another of the British painters whom Jennens patronised. The book on the table commemorates Jennens' Shakespeare editions (1770-4): its spine is labelled ' SHAKESPEAR WORKS'.

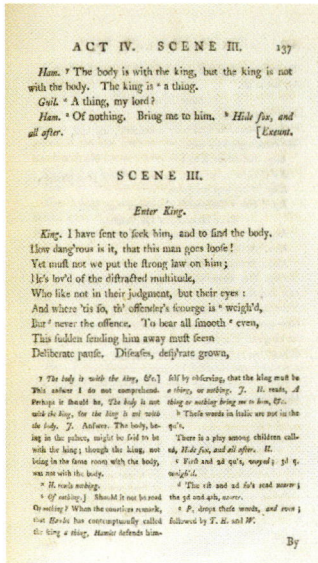

ACT IV.   SCENE III.   137

Ham. ⁷ The body is with the king, but the king is not with the body. The king is ⁸ a thing.

Guil. ⁹ A thing, my lord?

Ham. ⁿ Of nothing. Bring me to him. ᵇ *Hide fox, and all after.*   [*Exeunt.*

SCENE III.

Enter King.

King. I have sent to seek him, and to find the body.
How dang'rous is it, that this man goes loose!
Yet must not we put the strong law on him;
He's lov'd of the distracted multitude,
Who like not in their judgment, but their eyes :
And where 'tis so, th' offender's scourge is ᶜ weigh'd,
But ᵈ never the offence. To bear all smooth ᵉ even,
This sudden sending him away must seem
Deliberate pause. Diseases, desp'rate grown,

ROSENCRANTZ   My lord, you must tell us where the body is, and go with us to the King.

HAMLET   The body is with the King, but the King is not   25 with the body. The King is a thing.

14 **countenance** benevolent countenance, i.e. patronage
16 *****like an ape** as an ape does. Most editors (apart from Dover Wilson) regard
Q2's 'like an apple' as a misreading; Elze
comments that 'it may be surmised that
[Q1: 'as an Ape doth nuttes'] exhibits
the authentic words of the poet'; at all
events it presents an excellent and most
noteworthy reading', and Jenkins
remarks that the Q1 version 'shows how
well the actors understood'. Singer,
Staunton, Hudson and Rolfe actually
adopt the Q1 reading; some editors
(Oxf, Hibbard, Folg) adopt Farmer's
conjecture 'like an ape an apple'.
18–19 **When . . . again** The implication
is that the King will take back the benefits he has given at his convenience.
18 **gleaned** gathered, collected. This word
literally refers to the practice of gather-
ing ears of corn left after reaping as at
2.2.16: it is not normally used of the

sleeps i.e. is ineffective, does no harm
25–6 **The . . . body** 'This pretty piece of
chiasmus [the wordplay of reversing
the parallel terms *body* and *King*]
sounds impressive but is singularly
reluctant to yield up a sense that can be
apprehended by an audience in a theatre. Intended as a riddle, it remains a
riddle' (Hibbard). Jennens, however,
explains, 'The body, being in the
palace, might be said to be with the
king; though the king, not being in the
same room with the body, was not with
the body.' Hamlet might also mean that
the King is not with the body in the
sense that he is not (yet) dead. Other
editors suggest an allusion to the theo-
ry of the king's two bodies (natural and
political), whereby Hamlet casts doubt
on the legitimacy of this king, implying
that his kingship does not reside in his
physical body (see Jenkins, LN).
26–8 **The   nothing** The full stop after

Left: Jennens' edition of *Hamlet*, showing his innovative presentation of the text, with notes on the page. His reading of the lines at the top of this page answers a question about their sense, on which Samuel Johnson ('J'), George Steevens' collaborator, had declared himself baffled in his edition of 1765. *Right: The Arden Shakespeare: Hamlet*, ed. Ann Thompson and Neil Taylor (London, 2006), Act 4 scene 2. The editors endorse Jennens at several points. Here they cite his answer to Dr Johnson.

action. Most importantly, Jennens was the first editor of Shakespeare to give variant readings on the page. He was responding
to Edward Capell, whose recent edition (1768), the first involving
thorough collation of early texts, had not given evidence of that
collation, but had promised notes to follow, in separate volumes,
at a later date. Jennens thought that the student was entitled to
assess the editor's choice of reading by being provided with variants at the same time, and so he produced in effect the first
variorum edition of a Shakespeare play.

Received opinion would have us believe that Jennens was a
vain, ostentatious, insecure parvenu. But all the stories, still
repeated unquestioningly, of his pretension, his conspicuous
consumption and his being nicknamed 'Solyman the magnificent', originate with one man, a habitual liar who was a
byword even among his friends for professional jealousy and
malpractice: the editor George Steevens. When Jennens
brought out his *Lear* Steevens was working with Samuel
Johnson on a projected complete Shakespeare edition. Scholarly integrity was not among Steevens' priorities: he attacked
scholars publicly while plagiarising them, and altered Shake-

10   A VINDICATION

cant and unimportant. Among thefe are the following:

Shadowy,	al. *fhady.*	
You're,	al. *you are.*	
Churgeon,	al. *chirurgeon,*	al. *furgeon.*
To,	al. *into.*	
The entire,	al. *Th'intire.*	
Nere,	al. *never.*	
They'll,	al. *they will.*	

Now though fuch readings as thefe make no difference in the fenfe, they do in the meafure of the poetry; and, on that account, are not to be looked upon as intirely infignificant *.

                           Befides

* They ridicule our taking notice of various punctuation, and quote the following note,

    " There is no ftop in the qu's after *worth*; but in the fo's " is a period."

    But this is an unfair quotation, made by halves; for they have omitted that part of the note which fhews that the different pointing in this place is material: the whole note is as follows:

                           " There

OF KING LEAR.   11

Befides the above, there are other reafons why an editor of *Shakefpeare* fhould be exact in his collations. We have never yet had a correct edition of him; there are perpetual blunders in thofe of the greateft authority; and in fome cafes we are obliged, from letters put together, making no word, to guefs the word *Shakefpeare* meant. Now, though an editor, in thefe cafes, may be allowed to conjecture, yet it is his duty to give thefe mutilated readings, that the public may be indulged in their conjectures, as well as himfelf. In this view, fome readings that at prefent appear infignificant, may hereafter be affiftant to the critical conjecturer when any new difficulties may ftart; and on this account an editor may not, with fafety, omit any various reading, though ever fo trifling; becaufe he knows not what may, or what may not, become of ufe.

    " There is no ftop in the qu's after *worth*; but in the " fo's is a period, which feems to give the better fenfe. Upon " examining her own fincere heart, fhe finds her love equal " to her fifter's, nay greater."

                           Further,

---

speare's text in his own edition simply to call in question a rival editor's competence. Jennens' evidence-heavy edition was a thorn in his side.

    Steevens could find no ground to attack Jennens' scholarship, so he (absurdly) criticised his *Lear* for being 'minutely exact'. Unfortunately Jennens – always assertive in support of what he thought was the right way of doing something – produced a reply which was incontestable on scholarly grounds but which gave Steevens room to turn to mere ad hominem jibes (for example, sneering at the quality of his picture collection), rebutted by those who knew Jennens but repeated in biographical surveys by Steevens' associates. Hence the ruin of Jennens' reputation for the next two centuries.

In his *The Tragedy of King Lear, as lately published, Vindicated from the Abuse of the Critical Reviewers* (1772) Jennens asserts that even minor differences of punctuation and spelling can be significant in performance, and, until Shakespeare's text is reliably settled, a scrupulous editor should let the reader know of variants.

2

'Tis the just Providence of God, & I submit to it without murmuring'

POLITICS AND RELIGION

❧

JENNENS' LIFE was shaped by two deeply held allegiances, religious and political: to Protestant Christianity and to the deposed English royal family. In 1689 England changed its ruling dynasty, ousting the Catholic Stuart King James II and, subsequently, his Catholic descendants, in favour of the Protestant descendants of James' grandfather James I. This meant that in 1714 the Elector of Hanover became King George I, who could be shown to be only 58th in line to the British throne. Jennens was one of many English squires forced by the Roman Catholicism of James II and his heirs into an agonising conflict, between loyalty to the family which had the hereditary (and, many believed, divine) right to rule, and a desire to protect the Church of England and the English rule of law that was regarded as the backbone of the British constitution. Holders of professional or public office were required to abjure loyalty to the Stuarts and swear loyalty to the new regime. 'Non-jurors', those who refused or would refuse to take the oaths, excluded themselves from all political and ecclesiastical employment, such as priest, MP, magistrate, company director, government servant or army officer. Jennens' identity as a non-juror was our gain, for the lack of a professional role gave him leisure to foster the arts more actively than his wealth alone would have allowed.

Reactionary political views that Jennens may have inherited

Louis-François Roubiliac: *Religion* or *Christian Faith,* commissioned by Jennens to surmount the temple and monument which he erected at Gopsall to the memory of his friend Edward Holdsworth. The cross bears the phrase which (by tradition) prompted the conversion of Constantine, conventionally translated 'By this sign you shall conquer'. The scroll reads: 'the eternal gospel'; the base, 'The victory which conquered the world is our faith'. The cross bears the martyr's crown and palm. Jennens was perhaps expressing the earthly sacrifices, as well as the faith, of all non-jurors, himself as well as Holdsworth.

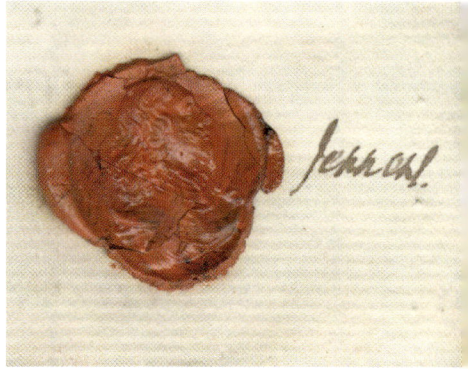

Left: A detail of the famous frontispiece of *Eikon Basilike* ('Image of the King', 1649 and much reprinted), the apologia for himself reputedly written by Charles I shortly before his execution; *Right:* Jennens' seal, copied from the image of the 'martyr king'. Unlike his successors, Charles I was both the rightful king and a high-church Anglican, which explains Jennens' choice.

from his mother's family and some staunch royalists among his uncles would have been encouraged at Oxford. His student days coincided with the alarmist aftermath of the 1715 Jacobite rebellion, when the university was enjoying a national reputation for unbridled pro-Stuart deviance. Non-jurors were not identical with Jacobites actively seeking to restore the Stuart dynasty, but Jennens' chosen college, Balliol, was especially notorious as being riddled with Jacobitism. Jennens did not graduate, which would have entailed taking the oaths. This is not in itself proof of non-juring allegiance, for eighteenth-century gentlemen's sons who had no need of a profession customarily attended the university without taking a degree. But the colour of Jennens' Oxford associates is attested by his lifelong friendship with, and support of, Edward Holdsworth, a classics fellow of Magdalen, who honourably resigned his fellowship rather than take the oaths; and by his correspondence with the scandalously Jacobite Dr William King, also of Balliol. Jennens later asked King to supply the epitaph for his monument to Holdsworth (now at Belgrave Hall Museum, Leicester). But in 1760 King changed sides, to Jennens' disgust, so Jennens wrote the epitaph himself, recording in it his outrage at King's behaviour. His own principles did not waver.

Non-jurors' political activity had to be either symbolic and polemical, or treasonable. Jennens steered an honourable course between subversion and passivity. Within the bounds of legality, he declared loyalty to the old regime. His seal portrayed the head of Charles I, and he collected, and displayed, a remarkable number of portraits of the Stuarts and their deposed descendants. Eighteenth-century collections of non-family portraits were assembled to represent the collector's pantheon of 'worthies'; contemporaries recognised this part of Jennens' collection as a statement of loyal adherence. He even had a piece of Charles II's oak, so called, built into the communion table in his chapel at Gopsall, and he crossed the names of the Hanoverian royal family out of the prayer books that he used there.

Jennens' choice of location in London, first in Queen Square and then in Great Ormond Street, may relate to his (and his brother-in-law Will Hanmer's) political–religious allegiance, in that it was at the heart of London non-juring terrain. Two of the most revered non-juring clergymen of the previous generation, George Hickes and Robert Nelson, had lived in Great Ormond Street, where they had established a noted oratory (venue for private worship). There were also oratories at Gray's Inn, at Bedford Court and at Scroop's Court, all in the immediate vicinity. While Jennens was living in Queen Square, he and the Hanmers had as their near neighbours some cousins by marriage, the Bowdlers, whose family was famous for adhering to non-juring principles right into the nineteenth century.

Being a non-juror did not necessarily mean cutting oneself off from the established church. Non-jurors were predominantly devout Anglicans and made a great contribution to the religious life of their time. Their devotional works went into multiple editions and were staple items of a serious library: for example, Robert Nelson's *Festivals and Fasts of the Church of*

One of a pair of very high-quality silver gilt-lined mugs, of apparently unique design, owned by Jennens, and displaying his allegiance: they bear the royal arms of France, three fleur-de-lys, which featured more prominently on the royal arms of the deposed British royal house of Stuart than on those of their Hanoverian successors. Presumably the mugs were used only among like-minded friends, to toast 'the king over the water'.

England (1704), which was on the library shelves at Gopsall, was in its twentieth edition by 1752. Their revival of early liturgies, and their emphasis on the significance of the Eucharist, constituted a major strand of eighteenth-century theology which has been seen as an anticipation of the Tractarian movement in the following century. Non-jurors stressed the mystical element in the Eucharist and its absolute centrality to Christian worship and belief.

Jennens himself was the patron of two livings and was a devoted member of the Anglican establishment. He lived at a time when many committed Anglicans felt their religion to be facing an unprecedented range of threats. They feared, with reason, that nonconformist churches and the anti-clerical government administration were undermining the strength of the established church. Moreover, they were alarmed by the inroads being made on Christian faith by scientific and Enlightenment rationalism and by newly rigorous biblical scholarship. 'The new philosophy put all in doubt': it caused the integrity of the Bible and the truth of the Christian revelation to be called into question, and made open contempt for religion a commonplace. This level of doubt and irreligion was as troubling a topic to thinking Britons as is terrorism or global warming in the twenty-first century, and it occupied even more column-inches in the broad-sheets.

When Jennens was twenty-eight a tragedy in his immediate family brought the spread of irreligion directly into his own life. His promising younger brother Robert, who had followed the family tradition of studying first at Oxford and then at the Inns of Court, cut his throat and threw himself out of the window of his rooms in Middle Temple. To Jennens this must have been more than the death of his brother by a sudden and horrible end. Christianity taught that in committing suicide, Robert had lost the hope of salvation. It transpired that he had died a victim of religious radicalism. He was found to have been in correspondence with another Oxford graduate, a professed sceptic, who gloated to Robert about the converts to disbelief that he had made. Robert was judged from this exchange of letters to have been preyed upon by doubt and, rather than becoming aggressively heretical like his correspondent, to have despaired and taken his own life.

Jennens had no truck with Enlightenment scepticism. Notwithstanding his respect for rigorous scholarship, he adhered to belief in the central Christian mysteries of revelation, resurrection and redemption. For him Christianity was the only sure foundation. Writing to Holdsworth about the new treatise on happiness written by his and Handel's friend James Harris, he reported that 'the Doctrine is Stoical: I confess I can draw no solid comfort from it, but am rather

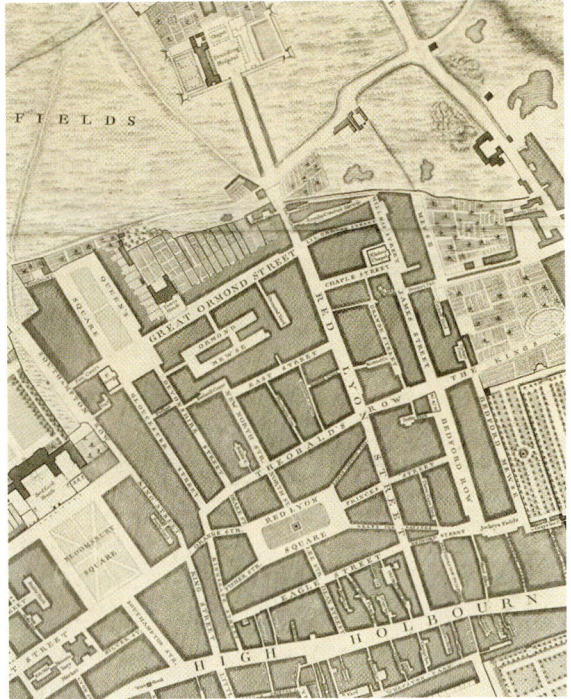

A section of John Rocque's map of 1746 showing Jennens' London environment. At the top is the Foundling Hospital site, surrounded by fields. Below to the left is Queen Square, where Jennens' brother-in-law lived. From its eastern lower corner runs Great Ormond St, where Jennens' house, on the north side, backed onto open country. Gray's Inn is lower right.

THE
ANCIENT LITURGY
OF THE
Church of Jerufalem,
BEING THE
LITURGY of St. JAMES,
Freed from all latter ADDITIONS and INTERPOLATIONS of what-
ever kind, and fo reftored to it's ORIGINAL PURITY:

By comparing it with the Account given of that LITURGY by

St. *Cyril* in his fifth MYSTAGOGICAL CATECHISM,
And with the CLEMENTINE LITURGY, *&c.*

Containing in fo many different Columns,

I. The Liturgy of St. *James* as we have it at prefent, the Interpolations being
only printed in a fmaller Character.
II. The fame Liturgy without thefe Interpolations, or the ancient Liturgy of
the Church of *Jerufalem.*
III. St. *Cyril's* Account of that Liturgy in his Vth Myftagogical Catechifm.
IV. The *Clementine* Liturgy.
V. So much of the correfponding Parts of the Liturgies of St. *Mark*, St. *Chryfoftom*
and St. *Bafil* as may ferve for illuftrating and confirming it.

WITH AN

Englifh TRANSLATION and NOTES,
AS ALSO

An APPENDIX, containing fome other ANCIENT PRAYERS,
Of all which an Account is given in the PREFACE.

Αὐτομαι λατεύω προφανὴς ὁ ψυχῇ μετὰ μεγίᾳ ἐιὼι θεὶς,—αλ—εὐχαριστοῦι ἐπὶ πᾶσι τῇ Θεῷ,—διὰ Προσφορᾶς
ἁγίας, δἰ εὐχῆς μακαρίας, αἰνέσεως, ὑμνῶν, εὐχαρισω, εὐλόγησιν, ἃ διαφέρᾳ οὐα τὸ Θεὶς κατ᾽ ἀδίαι λατρεία
ὃ τοιαῦτ ψυχῇ. Clem. Alex. Strom. vi. p. 797.

LONDON:
Printed by JAMES BETTENHAM. M.DCC.XLIV.

griev'd to find a Man of Parts neglecting his Bible for Heathen Philosophy.' His concern in his Shakespeare editions to render textual evidence accurately was a reflection of his Protestant belief in the paramount sanctity of the inspired Word of Scripture. He devoted much of his energy to the defence and spread of the Christian creed. His tomb, at Nether Whitacre in Warwickshire, records legacies to the Society for the Propagation of the Gospel in Foreign Parts (of which he was a member), a fund for lectures on the catechism, funds for the rebuilding of the church, and the return of parish tithes (from the Reformation onwards paid to the landowner) to the church. His picture collection contained an unusually high proportion of religious, especially biblical, subjects. Even the fireplaces of his mansion were adorned with reliefs of biblical scenes, a highly unusual choice of decoration. In the drawing room, flanked by cherubim, was the raising of Lazarus (based on an etching by Castiglione), and in the music room was Daniel in the lions' den – both traditionally symbolic of the cornerstone of Christian belief, the resurrection.

The evidence of Jennens' zealous, evangelising Christianity is at its most personal and complex in the iconography of his monument at Gopsall to

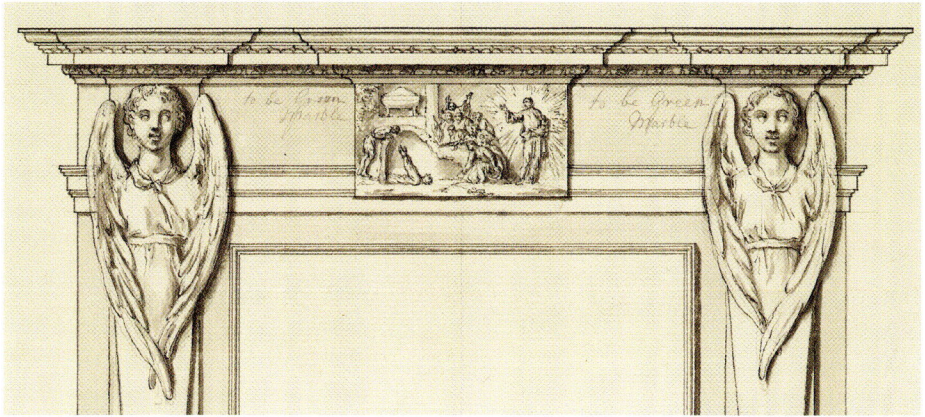

Holdsworth, who died in 1746. Positioned on rising ground, it formed a landmark for miles around, and consisted of a statue by the great sculptor Louis-François Roubiliac, surmounting a temple, within which was a cenotaph. The figure of Religion, or Christian Faith, which crowned the monument, is Roubiliac's only freestanding religious statue, and as an image was unprecedented in English sculpture. Jennens shaped the artist's expressiveness; he also provided the very telling inscriptions. The statue's cross bears the phrase which by tradition prompted the conversion of Constantine (an event of which Jennens had a picture in his collection). The other inscriptions are all quotations from the Bible: on the scroll, 'The eternal gospel'; round the base, 'The victory which conquered the world is our faith'; and on the frieze of the temple below, 'Thanks be to God who gives us the Victory through our Lord Jesus Christ' (used also in *Messiah*), with the addition, 'A temple of victory'. Jennens' Latin epitaph for Holdsworth suggests a dual meaning for this victory: eternal, over death, through Christian faith; and moral, ensuring fame on earth, through adherence to the Stuart cause. They are not easy victories. The statue carries the martyr's crown and palm. Jennens was perhaps expressing the sacrifices, as well as the faith, of all non-jurors, himself included.

Above: A design sketch for Gopsall Hall's drawing room chimney piece (which was realised), showing the centre panel reproduction of Giovanni Benedetto Castiglione's etching *The Raising of Lazarus* and annotated 'to be Green Marble'.

Opposite above: A sample of the rich theological contents of Jennens' library. He was one of the subscribers to this major work of the learned Bishop Rattray, in which the established church supported the non-juror movement to restore the Anglican liturgy to its 'ancient purity'. *Opposite below:* Jennens' monument to Holdsworth, from Nichols' *History of Leicestershire*.

July 25. 1744

Dear Sir

At my arrival in London, which was Yesterday, J immediately
perused the Act of the Oratorio with which you favour'd me,
and, the little time only J had it, gives me great Pleasure.
Your reasons for the Lenght of the first act are intirely
satisfactory to me, and it is likewise my Opinion to
have the following Acts short. J shall be very
glad and much obliged to you, if you will favour
me with the remaining Acts.   Be pleased
to point out these passages in te Messiah
which you think require altering.

J desire my humble Respects and thanks to
My Lord Guernsey for his many Civility's
to me.   and believe me to be with the greatest Respect

      Your
         most obedient and most humble
            servant
         George Frideric Handel

3

'I know of no Honour or Happiness in the world equal to the Friendship of a Virtuous Man'

FRIENDSHIP AND PHILANTHROPY

J ENNENS' LONG adult life was empty of close family rela-
tionships. His mother (his father's second wife) died when
he was only seven. His elder half-brother, his two younger
brothers and two of his three sisters died before he was thirty;
their father survived them, to the grand age of eighty-five.
Jennens' remaining sister moved with her husband to his family
estate in Flintshire. Their daughter Esther Hanmer gave
Jennens much happiness, and was to have inherited his properties, but she too predeceased him, and her son was heir to
the estates.

Jennens was lonely in Leicestershire, even prone to
periods of incapacitating misery, as his letters reveal. The
remarkable address given at his funeral dissects his tempera-
ment in a manner more akin to modern psychoanalysis than
eighteenth-century eulogy. The Rev. George Kelly specu-
lated that

> If any Part of his Conduct could be deemed exceptionable, it
> was in the Effects which naturally flow from an Impetuosity
> of Temper, by which I would be understood to mean some
> hasty Expressions which escaped him ... the rather the Effects
> of a natural Infirmity than a depraved Habit and Disposition
> of Mind; and seemed to proceed from a delicate Texture of the
> nervous System, too liable to Irritation; from whence arise
> violent Perturbations and Anxieties of the Mind, and not infre-
> quently an extreme Lowness and Depression of Spirits ... it is
> well known that he heartily bewailed this his Infirmity, and was

Handel to Jennens, 19 July 1744: Handel enthusiasti-cally acknowledges receipt of Jennens' libretto of Act 1 of *Belshazzar* and asks urgently for the rest; he also asks Jennens to point out those passages in *Messiah* which he thinks need altering. The polite expres-sions added in the signature lines ('with the greatest respect', 'and most humble'), clearly squashed in as afterthoughts, show him anxious to retain Jennens' friendship and collaboration.

Friend to both Handel and Jennens, James Harris (1709-80) was a cousin of Handel's patron the 4th Earl of Shaftesbury, and the intellectual heir of his philosopher uncle the 3rd Earl. In his own work on aesthetics he praised Handel's imitative word-setting. He was the principal librettist of Handel's *L'Allegro, Il Penseroso ed Il Moderato*, which Jennens encouraged and on which he collaborated, writing the words of *Il Moderato*.

frequently angry with himself on this account, much more so than with those he seemed to chide.

He was also reportedly shy, especially in mixed company. He never married. Evidently he was not, as we would say now, very comfortable in his own skin.

The friendship of like-minded men was his solace. He was one of the 'brother Handelists' who included James Harris (with whom he collaborated on *L'Allegro*, and to whose sadly short-lived son John Thomas he stood godfather), the 4th Earl of Shaftesbury (Harris' cousin and Handel's patron), Sir Wyndham Knatchbull (Harris' brother-in-law and a fellow student of Jennens at Balliol) and Lord Radnor (like Jennens, the owner of a collection of manuscript copies of music by Handel). The Harris family's lively correspondence shows them reporting to each other Jennens' shared or contrary opinions of performances that they attended with him, and his occasional insider information, gleaned from Handel, about forthcoming musical events.

Handel and Jennens remained lifelong friends despite their similar irascibility, Handel bequeathing Jennens two excellent pictures and Jennens commissioning the 'Gopsall' portrait of Handel from Hudson (1756; see p. 48). The freedom with which Jennens criticised Handel when he thought Handel was not doing his best – akin to the exasperation of a schoolmaster over the slackness of a brilliant but intransigent pupil – was received sometimes with particular politeness, as in the letter in which Handel, wanting another libretto from Jennens, asks which passages in *Messiah* he should amend, and squashes extra expressions of respect into his signature lines. But they also talked as frank equals, as in the exchange which Jennens

it was with the greatest Pleasure I saw the Continuation of Your Kindness by the Lines You was pleased to send me, in order to be crefix'd to Your Oratorio Messiah, which I set to Musick before I left England. I am emboldned, Sir, by the generous Concern You please to take in relation to my affairs, to give You an Account of the Success I have met here. The Nobility did me the Honour to make among themselves a Subscription for 6 Nights which did fill a Room of 600 Persons, so that I needed not sell one single Ticket at the door. and without Vanity the Performance was received with a general Approbation. Sigra Avolio which I brought with me from London pleases extraordinary, I have formed an other Tenor Voice which gives great Satisfaction, the Bases and Counter Tenors are very good, and the rest of the Chorus Singers (by my Direction) do exceeding well, as for the Instruments

Handel to Jennens, 29 December 1741: after opening his first concert series in Dublin with *L'Allegro, Il Penseroso ed Il Moderato*, Handel writes Jennens one of his longest surviving letters, acknowledging the epigraphs Jennens has sent him for the wordbook of 'your oratorio *Messiah*' (premiered Dublin 13 April 1742), and, 'emboldened by the generous concern you please to take in relation to my affairs', sharing news of his success.

It was indeed Your humble Servant which intended You a visit in my way from Ireland to London, for I certainly could have given you a better Account by word of mouth, as by writing, however Your Messiah was received in that Country, yet as a Noble Lord, and no less then the Bishop of Elphin (a Nobleman very learned in musick) has given his observations in writing of this Oratorio, I send You here annexed the contents of it in his own words.—

pass'd Coventry You may easily imagine, Sir, that I should not have neglected of paying my Respects to him, since you know the particular Esteem I have for His Lordship. I think it a very long time to the month of November next when I can have some hopes of seeing You here in Town. Pray let me hear mean while of Your Health and Welfare, of which I take a real Share being with an uncommon Sincerity and Respect

Handel to Jennens, 9 September 1742: *Above:* On his way back to London from Ireland, Handel had hoped to call on Jennens at Gopsall to share news of 'how well your Messiah was received in that country'. *Below:* in concluding his letter, Handel thinks it 'a very long time to the month of November next when I can have some hopes of seeing you here in Town', and asks for news of Jennens' 'Health and Welfare, in which I take a real Share'.

Jennens' friend Edward Holdsworth was the leading Virgil scholar of his day. While Holdsworth was working abroad, Jennens encouraged, helped with, promoted, and saw through the press Holdsworth's explication of a knotty point in Virgil studies, much discussed in their letters. Holdsworth wanted to name him on the title page, but Jennens demurred, hence 'Letters to a Friend'.

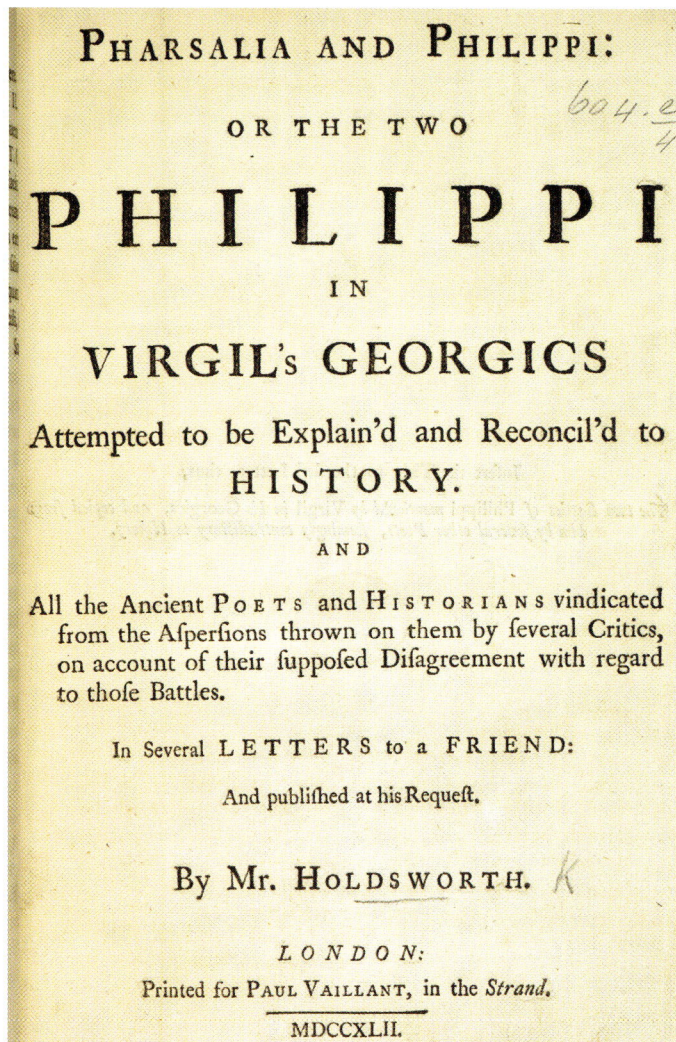

PHARSALIA AND PHILIPPI:

604.e
4

OR THE TWO

PHILIPPI

IN

VIRGIL's GEORGICS

Attempted to be Explain'd and Reconcil'd to
HISTORY.

AND

All the Ancient POETS and HISTORIANS vindicated
from the Aspersions thrown on them by several Critics,
on account of their supposed Disagreement with regard
to those Battles.

In Several LETTERS to a FRIEND:

And published at his Request.

By Mr. HOLDSWORTH.

LONDON:
Printed for PAUL VAILLANT, in the *Strand*.
MDCCXLII.

recorded in the margin of his copy of Mainwaring's biography of Handel (1760):

> Handel told me that the words of Il Trionfo &c. were written by Cardinal Pamphilii, & added 'an old Fool!' I ask'd 'why Fool? because he wrote an Oratorio? perhaps you will call me fool for the same reason!' He answer'd 'So I would, if you flatter'd me, as He did'.

Handel's two surviving letters to Jennens from his Irish sojourn (1741–2) show a real pleasure in sharing with Jennens the good news of his success, of the Irish audience's gratifying response to their collaborations, and of the risible efforts of competitors in London. Handel even seems to have made a detour to Gopsall on his way back to London from Dublin especially to tell him all about it (but Jennens was away from home, so Handel wrote to him instead).

Jennens was constantly concerned to foster Handel's career. 'Mr Jennens' is listed as a subscriber in all Handel's works published by subscription, ordering two or more copies during the 1730s. He designed *Messiah* to be performed for Handel's profit. His practical generosity was legendary among those who knew of it, but, said the Rev. Kelly at his funeral,

> He was never heard to boast of the Favours he had bestowed, or to reproach the Receiver with an imprudent Use of his Benefits, however justly he might have been induced to it; observing that most excellent Precept of our Lord, Not to let his left Hand know what his right Hand did.

Jennens' burial monument, in the family church of Nether Whitacre, Warwickshire, with a tablet erected by his nephew and executors detailing his many bequests to charities, which amounted (in 21st-century terms) to over £1 million.

His uncle Sir John Cotton had been the leading patron of the non-juring laity in his generation, and Jennens took up that role in his turn. To Thomas Bedford – deprived clergyman, scholar, and chaplain to Cotton – he gave the job of cataloguing the library at Gopsall, for a substantial fee. He had Holdsworth's *Letters* on Virgil printed by William Bowyer, the

non-juring son of a non-juror, both of whom specialised in issuing non-jurors' publications. The Rev. Dr Robert Gordon, the leading non-juring divine of his generation and the last in the true succession of non-juring bishops dating from the time of the 1689 Revolution, lived in cramped circumstances off Theobalds Road, not far from Jennens' Great Ormond Street residence; there Jennens gave house-room to Gordon's book collection and, through Holdsworth, helped to amplify it with foreign publications.

His charity extended beyond immediate friends. Welfare in eighteenth-century England depended on private philanthropy. Besides being a regular donor, Jennens bequeathed £500 each to six London hospitals, £200 each to the girls' orphanage and the home for former prostitutes in London, £1000 to schools around Gopsall and £300 to the poor of local villages (multiply by 180 for modern equivalents).

With his friend Edward Holdsworth (1684–1746) Jennens shared a political alignment, though Holdsworth was probably, unlike Jennens, actively political. He was suspected of being a Jacobite agent – one of his post-Oxford occupations, taking young gentlemen on the Grand Tour, was a common cover for subversive activity – and his correspondence with Jennens was regularly opened by British government spies. The friends enjoyed teasing the intelligence services by planting archly knowing remarks in their letters in extra-clear handwriting.

Professionally, Holdsworth was a noted classicist, especially esteemed for his understanding of Virgil, and from 1736 until their publication in 1742 Jennens was the driving force behind Holdsworth's *Letters* on a knotty point of Virgil scholarship, the apparent inconsistency in the location of Philippi. Having suggested the project, he energetically contributed references, criticisms and emendations to the work in progress. These show breadth and depth of reading, competence in Greek and Latin, and a characteristic determination to establish critical truth through scholarly exactness. In Holdsworth's absence abroad he saw the book through the press, watched its fortunes in the shops and advised on the wisdom of a second edition. This form of loyal service to his friend continued after Holdsworth's death, when Jennens co-operated in the publication in 1768 of Holdsworth's complete *Dissertation and Remarks on Virgil*.

Working as a freelance tutor after resigning his fellowship, Holdsworth was, compared with Jennens, poor: a situation that Jennens treated with sensitivity as well as generosity (contrary to the image put about by Steevens). Their correspondence shows him paying off Holdsworth's debts; handling his financial affairs for him; giving him maps he had

Jennens in later life, by Nathaniel Dance-Holland (1735-1811). Like many contemporary British artists, and like many patronised by Jennens, Dance studied in Italy. On his return he became a successful portrait painter, and was a founder of the Royal Academy. In later life, adding a patroness' name to his own, he became a politician and was for many years MP for East Grinstead.

enquired about ('for how do I know but some time or other we may both make use of 'em together?'); refusing payment for a book he had asked for; giving him a horse when he needed fresh air and exercise; and providing London accommodation when he needed somewhere to stay (including his own bed and his wine cellar), all without a hint of patronage or condescension – rather the reverse. When Holdsworth expresses his obligation for the last of these services, Jennens replies: 'Trespassing upon Civility is language I don't understand among Friends. I think myself oblig'd to your Friendship that you will make use of my lodgings or any thing else that belongs to me.'

The letters between them are full of expressions of warm regard for Holdsworth's friendship and integrity, most of them tactfully reticent and all of them delicate. One of the epigraphs to *Saul* focuses on the relationship between David and Jonathan, citing Cicero's *De amicitia* to the effect that the basis of true friendship is virtue. Jennens told Holdsworth that he

All his papers of this kind were, on his decease, in 1746, left by Mr. Holdsworth, to his most intimate friend, Charles Jennens, Esq; of Copthall, in Leicestershire; who was so kind as to put them into my hands, at my earnest request; that so great a treasure might not be lost to the world.

SAUL,

AN

ORATORIO;

OR,

SACRED DRAMA.

As it is Perform'd

At the KING's THEATRE in the Hay-Market.

Set to Mufick by GEORGE-FREDERIC HANDEL, Efq;

'Αρετη ποιευ φιλον ὁςις ἀρις Θ..　Aur. Carm.

Qui autem in virtute fummum bonum ponunt, præclarè illi quidem : Sed hæc ipfa virtus Amicitiam & gignit & Continet : Nec fine virtute Amicitia effe ullo pacto poteft. Cic.

LONDON:

Printed for THO. WOOD, and Sold by THO. ASTLEY, in St. *Paul's Church-yard*, J. SHUCKBURGH, at the *Inner-Temple-Gate*, and at the KING's THEATRE in the *Hay-Market*. 1738.

[Price One Shilling.]

The title page of Jennens' wordbook (libretto) for Handel's *Saul*. Jennens told Holdsworth that he selected its epigraphs from authoritative classical writers (one Greek, one Roman) 'to point out more strongly my own Sentiments express'd in some parts of the Oratorio'. Their message is that a virtuous friendship is one of life's greatest blessings. The Greek motto is from the Carmen Aureum, a moral poem thought in Jennens' day to be by Pythagoras: 'Whoever is outstanding in virtue, make him your friend'. The Latin motto is from Cicero's dialogue *De amicitia*, a favourite eighteenth-century text: 'Now, there are those who locate the "chief good" in virtue, and that is a noble doctrine. But this very virtue is the parent and preserver of friendship, and without virtue friendship cannot possibly exist.'

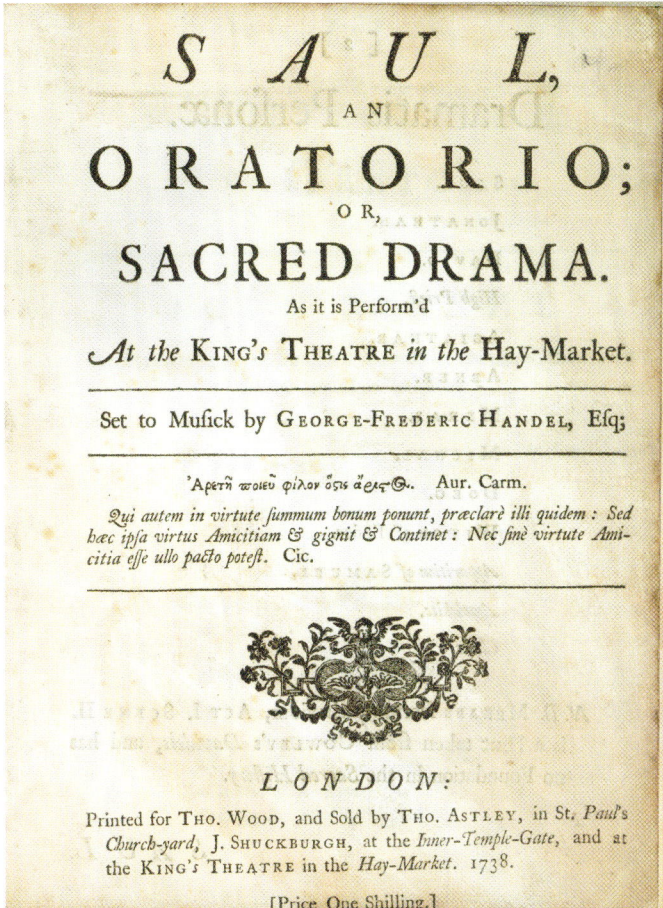

chose the epigraphs 'to point out more strongly my sentiments express'd in some parts of the oratorio'. He unburdened himself unreservedly to Holdsworth, perhaps the more readily because their contact was mainly by letter. Jennens' regard for Holdsworth, and his ways of expressing it, form a signal testimony to the emotional capacity of friendship in the eighteenth century.

4

'I ... neither have nor pretend to have the least Tast in Architecture'

CULTIVATING THE VISUAL ARTS

❧

I N 1740 Jennens viewed the recently erected New Building, which his friend Holdsworth had designed for his old Oxford college, Magdalen (and which still stands). He wrote to Holdsworth that he admired it, but added, 'I ... neither have nor pretend to have the least Tast [sic] in Architecture'. As often with deprecating disclaimers of the time, this was not entirely true. Jennens transformed the seventeenth-century Leicestershire house in which he had grown up, and which he inherited in 1747, into what Nikolaus Pevsner called England's 'last great example of Palladian architecture'. It was a building of distinctive idiosyncrasy, and Jennens' taste was what shaped it.

Gopsall Hall no longer stands. It was pulled down in 1951. Its last owner had let it run down and army occupation during World War II further degraded it. Thieves stole the lead off the roof the night after the government buildings inspector had judged it to be just viable for restoration, after which it was deemed too expensive to save.

The house that Jennens built was extended in the late nineteenth century (for royal visits), and our understanding of its development is based on a few depictions dating from just after its completion and a remarkable set of 89 designs now in the Royal Institute of British Architects (RIBA) Library Drawings and Archives Collections. These designs throw up a number of questions about Gopsall. They are by several hands and

Gopsall Hall south front depicted in 1881 by Alfred Grey (1845-1926) and viewed through the ruins of Jennens' 'temple' to his friend Edward Holdsworth, designed by James Paine, which formerly housed Holdsworth's cenotaph and was surmounted by Louis-François Roubiliac's statue of Religion (see p. 18). The ruins are still visible at Gopsall.

Gopsall Hall as constructed by Jennens. This charming view of the south front, painted by an unknown artist some time after 1764, shows, at left, Jennens' monument to Holdsworth, crowned by the statue of Religion which he commissioned from Roubiliac (see p. 12).

many of them are unsigned. They show a series of rethinkings of the possible layout of the new house, but are mostly undated, so a clear sequence cannot be reliably made out. What is clear is that they suggest a client intending to impose his own idiosyncratic ideas, and developing them over many years, perhaps several decades, for some of the designs are more in the style of the 1720s and 1730s than the 1740s.

From the later eighteenth century onwards various sources attribute the design of Gopsall Hall, or early versions of it, to John Westley, a Leicester builder-carpenter, and the final and implemented design to the Hiorn brothers, William and David, prominent West Midlands builder-architects. It was only when Jennens came to plan the garden buildings, notably the temple to Holdsworth, that he employed an architect with a national reputation. James Paine was based in London, whilst Westley and the Hiorn brothers were local men. The Hiorns could be relied on to oversee the work regularly when Jennens was in London, and were at hand when Jennens was at home, so they could be responsive to the needs of an amateur enthusiast. They were moreover known to, and worked for, Jennens' family and friends: for his cousin and executor Sir Robert

Burdett at Foremark Hall, Derbyshire, and in Warwickshire for his cousin Lord Guernsey at Packington and his neighbour Sir Roger Newdigate at Arbury. The way in which this group shared expertise is suggested by the advisory visit to Gopsall in October 1748 of Sanderson Miller (for whom William Hiorn worked as mason) at the recommendation of Lord Guernsey.

Gopsall Hall was already nearing completion when the consultant engineer John Grundy visited it in 1750. He had provided a design for the grounds in 1749, which shows the outline of the house; his description of the house in his travel journal indicates that this outline was actual, not speculative. His record was unknown to the compilers of the RIBA drawings catalogue, who had assumed

This detail of John Grundy's magnificent plan for the laying out of Gopsall's grounds (not realised) shows that the hall already had its final outlines in 1749 (south is at the top).

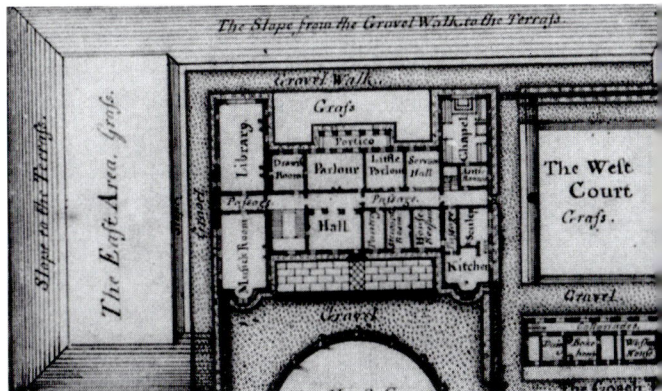

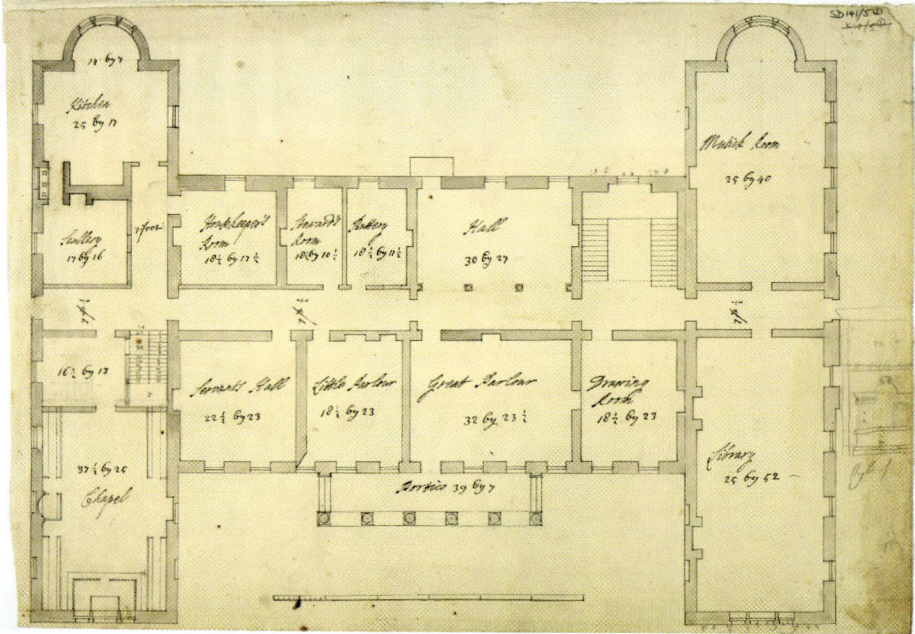

One of several drawings for Gopsall Hall in the RIBA collection labelled by Jennens himself. The three largest rooms are the music room, library and chapel – all additions to the original manor house.

that building began only at the death of Jennens' father in 1747. But the Grundy evidence makes that virtually impossible: the house cannot have been created to the point of being partly furnished in two building seasons. That being so, rebuilding must have started while Jennens' father was still alive, and the earlier designs may have been made at his instigation. They incorporate more of the old house than remained in the final construct, but a 'ghost' of the old house's core seems to have been preserved. The demolition of the house means that we now cannot tell how much old fabric was retained.

The RIBA designs and the completed project are characteristic of Jennens in that they are atypical for the period, suggesting a creator intent on arriving at the solution that seemed right to him, regardless of the dictates of tradition, fashion or even decorum. In that respect Jennens was perhaps right to say he had no taste in architecture. He (or his father?) had subscribed to James Gibbs' *Book of Architecture* (1728), which was specially intended for 'such Gentlemen as might be

A selection of drawings for Gopsall Hall's interiors showing Jennens' eclecticism: clockwise from top left: rococo dining room chimney-piece and over-mantel; chinoiserie bridge; gothick summerhouse; regency reading desk for the chapel (annotated by Jennens in two languages 'or rather pulpit').

concerned in Building, especially in the remote parts of the Country, where little or no assistance from Designs can be procured', and which is sometimes cited as a source for the Gopsall designs; but Gibbs has no examples of Gopsall's balustraded portico or apsed wings. What we know of Gopsall's development suggests a client–contractor relationship rather special to its time and place, in which the client was a major source of ideas.

On some of the RIBA drawings showing later stages of the design development Jennens has labelled the rooms (differently on different drawings). Two main elements are obvious, and significant. One is that almost from the start of the planning the existing house was to be enlarged by adding two large rooms to each end, making an H-shape of the whole; and three of these four rooms reflect Jennens' main interests in life. They were a library, a chapel, and a music room (the fourth was the kitchen). Furthermore, adding these rooms but leaving much of the old core's layout intact resulted in an extraordinarily old-fashioned and democratic arrangement, whereby, for example, access to the chapel ran past the servants' quarters. The notion that Jennens was vain and proud is here again contradicted by the evidence of his way of life. Contemporaries were perhaps misled by outward grandeur. For some aspects of the renovation of Gopsall, no expense was spared. The interiors were sumptuous: for example, the chapel was panelled entirely in cedarwood. According to the Leicestershire historian John Nichols, who knew Jennens, laying out the grounds reputedly cost the equivalent in modern terms of around £50 million.

In his role of 'improver' as in his musical tastes, Jennens was receptive to contemporary developments. The rococo designs for Gopsall's exquisite plasterwork and furniture draw on Chippendale's newly published *The Gentleman and Cabinet-Makers Director* (1754), and the elaborate pulpit in the otherwise sober chapel looks forward to the Regency. Once the house was complete, Jennens rejected the plan for the grounds drawn by Grundy in 1749 in favour of a much less formal

One of the paintings in Jennens' collection: *The Infant Christ Asleep on the Cross*, attributed to Bartolomé Estebán Murillo (Spanish, 1618-82), one of his several versions of this complex religious subject and probably dating from the 1670s (now in the Graves Art Gallery, Sheffield). Uniting the nativity with a foretelling of the crucifixion, it forms a visual analogue of Jennens' libretto of *Messiah*. To collect paintings on religious, especially New Testament, themes was unusual in mid-18th-century England and would have been considered a sign of papist tendencies; the large number of religious paintings in Jennens' collection testifies to his individualism and High Anglicanism.

parkscape. He was a subscriber to William Chambers' *Designs of Chinese Buildings* (1757), but already in 1749 he had a boat-house with Chinese decoration. He was equally responsive to gothick, exemplified in a pinnacled summerhouse.

The RIBA designs for Gopsall's dining room and drawing room interiors show the provision of decorative plasterwork frames spaced along the walls, and the design for the former is inscribed 'the Pannels plain, being to be covered with valuable Paintings'. Jennens had begun to form his collection of paint-ings, sculpture, prints and drawings by the 1730s, and by 1766 the paintings and sculptures alone numbered over five hundred items. In that year they were listed in Thomas Martyn's *The English Connoisseur*, a survey of the country's leading art collec-tions in public and private hands. Jennens' was one of only four commoners' collections to be included and by far the largest of all the picture collections surveyed. It exemplifies contempo-rary advanced tastes, both in old masters and modern art – but not those of a culture slave. A manuscript of sales catalogues in the Victoria and Albert Museum suggests that he was neither bound by fashion nor using art as an investment. Nor was he just picking up what was most readily available. For example, one had to make an effort to secure a good Claude, and he had a pair of Claude landscapes, described by a nine-teenth-century cataloguer as 'capitally fine'.

To acquire Italian works, such as Jennens' Carraccis, Marrattis and Guidos, a continental agent was almost essential. Some English artists working in Italy acted as such. Possibly James Russel, who lived in Rome, whose politically like-minded father Jennens helped financially, and who painted Holdsworth's portrait (p. 26), put him in the way of acquiring some of the Italian items in his collection. Jennens' enthusiasm for things Italian is apparent in another aspect of his collection: he patronised British artists when they were fresh from expo-sure to Italian influence, such as Richard Wilson, from whom he bought an Italian landscape, William Hoare, to whom he appears to have sat for a portrait in 1738, and Richard

MAIN PORTION.

By Direction of the Right Hon. EARL HOWE, G.C.V.O.

GOPSALL, LEICESTERSHIRE.

Shackerstone two miles.   Ashby-de-la-Zouch eight miles.

CATALOGUE
OF THE
Fine Antique and Modern

Furniture in the Mansion

WHICH INCLUDES

FENDERS, IMPLEMENTS, CURTAINS,
PERSIAN, INDIAN, TURKEY AND PILE CARPETS AND RUGS,
BEDSTEADS AND BEDDING, including

A PRINCE CHARLES STATE BEDSTEAD
with the Stuart Tartan Silk Drapery,

SETS OF COUCHES, SETTEES, EASY, LOUNGE, AND STANDARD CHAIRS,

Writing Tables,	Side Tables,	Commodes,	Court Cupboards,
Screens,	Cabinets,	Sideboards,	Buffet,
Torchieres,	Secretaires,	Wardrobes,	Armoires,

and Mirrors in Very Choice Carved Frames.

COLLECTION OF PICTURES,

English, Dutch, etc., Schools by Eminent Old Masters, including a Series relating to
the Pretender Period,

Engravings, Prints, and Drawings,
GRANDFATHER, MANTEL & BRACKET CLOCKS IN CHOICE CASES,
A FEW ORNAMENTS,

THE EXTENSIVE LIBRARY OF BOOKS,
BILLIARD TABLE & ACCESSORIES by COX & YEMAN,

The Usual Furnishings of the Bedchambers & Domestic Apartments, Garden Vases, Summer
House, a Station 'Bus, a Wagonette and a Brougham, Harness, a Manual Fire Engine
and Appliances.

Messrs. TROLLOPE

Having Sold the Estate, will Sell the above by Auction, on the Premises,
On MONDAY, 14th OCTOBER, 1918, and Following Days,
At Twelve o'clock precisely.

ON VIEW: PRIVATELY, by Catalogue and Card only, on THURSDAY; and PUBLICLY,
by Catalogue, on the FRIDAY and SATURDAY preceding the Sale. Catalogues to admit
to View (1/- each) and Card for Private View may be had at the Auctioneers' Offices—

25, MOUNT STREET, GROSVENOR SQUARE, W. 1;

Hobart Place, Eaton Square, S.W. 1;
West Halkin Street, Belgrave Square, S.W. 1; and } LONDON.
5, Victoria Street, Westminster, S.W. 1.

Telephone Nos :

Gopsall Hall dispersed: auction catalogue of the contents of Gopsall Hall, October 1918. Denying later researchers a wealth of information, the contents of Gopsall Hall were abysmally catalogued when they were mostly sold off in a local auction during the financial difficulties that afflicted many landowners toward the end of World War I. The greater part of Jennens' 'Extensive library of books' is tantalisingly listed in such terms as 'theological works, 25 volumes'.

Hayward, who worked on the sculpture at Gopsall. Later in life he was in the vanguard of the movement to encourage talent cultivated at home, and was an early appreciator of members of the St Martin's Lane School. Most individually, and again expressive of the man, his collection was often remarked on by contemporaries for its high proportion of religious subjects, and its pantheon of Jacobite royalty (see chapter 2). Jennens' collection was as much a missionary statement of belief and a proclamation of allegiance as a vehicle for patronage and an expression of taste.

5

'Insist on the whole Scores being copy'd'

CULTIVATING MUSIC

The 3rd Earl of Aylesford (1715–77), the son of Jennens' cousin Mary Fisher, an amateur violinist and the inheritor of Jennens' great music collection; a portrait attributed to Gainsborough. At Oxford in 1733 he was one of the student orators at the Encaenia (degree celebrations), which Jennens attended and at which Handel premiered his oratorio *Athalia*, containing music derived from the Scarlatti manuscripts that he had borrowed from Jennens.

(*Below*) For John Walsh jr's folio publication of the full score of Handel's *Alexander's Feast* (1738) Jennens ordered more copies than any other subscriber.

JENNENS WAS A self-confessed Handel addict. He (or in early years just possibly his father) was a subscriber, sometimes for multiple copies, to all Handel's works published by subscription. Handel's music was his only bulwark against recurring depression: when Handel was ill, he found that 'the Town has lost its only Charm'. He was constantly eager for Handel's success, as Handel himself acknowledged (letter of 9 June 1744); he even said, with reference to Handel's scriptural works, 'Everything that has been united with Handel's music becomes sacred by such a union in my eyes', an extraordinary statement for a devout Christian. From the 1740s onwards, aiming at a comprehensive collection of Handel's music, he commissioned manuscript copies from Handel's circle of copyists. They formed the core of his stellar collection of music manuscripts and early editions, known as the Aylesford Collection after his young cousin Lord Guernsey (later the 3rd Earl of Aylesford), to whom he bequeathed it. Dispersed in auction sales in 1873 and 1918, a large part of the collection was subsequently redeemed and is now in

H

Rt. Hon. Lady Charlotte Hyde.
Iohn Hunter, Efq.
James Hunter, Efq.
Philip Hubert, Efq.
Robert Holden, Efq.
James Harris. Efq.
Mr. Samuel Hoole.
Mr. Iohn Harris, Organ Builder.
Mr. Wm. Hayes, of Oxon.
The Revd Mr. Wm. Harrington.
Mr. James Hefletine, Organift of Durham.

I

Charles Jennens, Efq. Six Books.
Ralph Jennifon, Efq.

K

Her Grace the Dutchefs of Kent.
Sir Windham Knatchbull Bart. Two Books
Mr. Samuel King.
Mr. Keeble.

at the Crown and Anchor Mufical Society at Exeter

N

O

Leake Okeover, Efq.

P

Rt. Hon. Countefs of Peml
Five Books.
Tho! Pitt, Efq.
George Pitt, Efq.
Tho! Prouce, Efq.
Philarmonic Society, Two Colonel Poultney.
Mr. Palmer.
Mr. Iohn Pigott, Organift Windfor.

Q

His Grace the Duke of Q berry.

A sample of Jennens' music collection: Handel's *Brockes Passion* (1716) sets the German Passion oratorio text by the poet Barthold Heinrich Brockes (1680-1747) in the Lutheran tradition. Jennens had it copied for his collection without text, intending to supply it with English words (perhaps hoping for performance in Britain), but in the event completing only a few pages. This page shows the Evangelist's first recitative, with text added in Jennens' hand.

many libraries around the world, notably the Henry Watson Music Library (Manchester Public Libraries).

But Jennens was not a one-composer fanatic. He subscribed to others' compositions too, both British and foreign. He had catholic but decisive musical tastes. He shared his contemporaries' enthusiasm for sampling the new. The names of over thirty Italian composers in the Aylesford Collection attest to the breadth of his musical interests. Holdsworth was invaluable in sending him music from Italy, which frequently entailed having manuscripts specially copied. Jennens' desire for completeness in collecting composers besides Handel is evident in Holdsworth's reassurance in 1733 that 'Monsr la Cene who has publish'd Vivaldi's & Albinoni's works assur'd me that if you have 12 of Vivaldi's op. and 9 of Albinoni, you have all.'

Of Italian operas, 'insist on the whole Scores being copy'd,'

Jennens instructed Holdsworth in 1741, meaning to have recitatives copied as well as arias, 'that if they deserve we may have them perform'd on the English Stage'. This impetus to produce something tangible, and to communicate rather than passively to enjoy, is characteristic. (A similar urge may be expressed in his copy of Handel's setting (1716) of the Passion text by the German poet Barthold Heinrich Brockes, which had no prospect of being performed in Britain; Jennens had it copied without its German text and started to give it English text underlay.) But judgement prevails: 'By what I have seen of the Italian Operas you sent me', he writes subsequently,

> they seem to be of the usual stamp, very defective both in Judgement & Invention, contriv'd without Art, & executed without Spirit; the Harmony thin; the Airs dry & inexpressive, yet capricious; passages frequently repeated, tho' tiresome at the first hearing; & all this stuff intermix'd with such long tedious Recitative, that I think I could not bear to sit out one of the Italian Operas, or if I did, it must be for Penance, not for Entertainment.

This dismissal makes Holdsworth diffident about a subsequent purchase, actually one of his major acquisitions for Jennens:

> I have bought for you above 150l weight of musick, enough to fill a large box, wch I have order'd to be sent wth Mr Pitt's things. I mention the weight, because as you know I am perfectly ignorant of musick, I thought it the best way to buy it as some people do Libraries by the pound, and take my

Handel responds (on 30 September 1749) to Jennens' request, received the previous day, for a specification for the organ to be installed in the Gopsall Hall music room. The letter shows their continuing amiable relationship after their oratorio collaboration ended. The resulting organ was inherited by Lord Aylesford and is now at the Aylesford estate church, St James, Great Packington.

A piano comes to England: Holdsworth, in Florence (9 August 1732), reports the despatch to Jennens of one of the first pianos to reach England (workshop of Bartolomeo Cristofori), and ends his letter by promising to send 'a book of Sonatas compos'd here purposely for the Pianoforte' – probably Lodovico Giustini's *Sonate da cimbalo di piano e forte detto volgarmente di martelletti*, op. 1 (Florence, 1732), said to be the first music written for the piano.

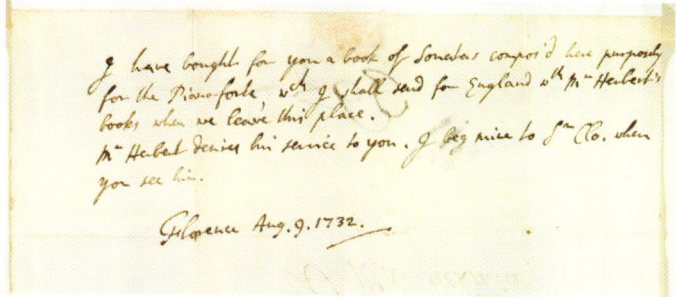

[handwritten letter reproduced:]

J have bought for you a book of Sonatas compos'd here purposely for the Piano-forte, wch J shall send for England wth Mr Herbert's books when we leave this place.
Mr Herbert desires his service to you. J beg mine to Sr Clo. when you see him.

Florence Aug. 9. 1732.

chance whether it prov'd good or bad. All that I can say of it is that 'tis part of Cardinal Ottoboni's collection; And most of it by celebrated hands, such as Scarlatti, Pollaroli, Mancini, Bencini, and Marcello. And the purchase not very great; the whole amounting to not above 40 shillings, besides the expences of sending it home, so that in case it shou'd prove as bad as the rest you have from hence 'twill be almost worth the money for ye Housekeeper to put under pyes. And one comfort is, that shou'd it fall into the hands of the Spaniards, the loss wou'd not be very deplorable. Since Baron d'Astorga is one of your favourites I am sorry his name was not amongst the others. But his compositions are scarce at Rome, and notwithstanding I enquir'd often for him, I never cou'd meet with any more of his pieces than those I sent you.

Jennens suspends his customary scepticism because Ottoboni's former patronage of Handel bespeaks good taste, and when the box arrives he writes to Holdsworth (17 January 1743):

> I told you before that one of the Composers in my Box was good, I mean Scarlatti: & I shall not condemn the rest without a fair Trial. Handel has borrow'd a dozen of the Pieces, & I dare say I shall catch him stealing from them; as I have formerly, both from Scarlatti & Vinci.

Handel had indeed drawn on manuscripts of works by Scarlatti and Vinci that Jennens had loaned him, as modern scholarship has shown.

Jennens appears to have been a proficient keyboard player. He took a lively interest in the keyboard instruments that Handel commissioned for the oratorio season in which he premiered *Saul* and *Israel in Egypt*. A report by an early visitor to the rebuilt Gopsall Hall provides a fascinating picture of

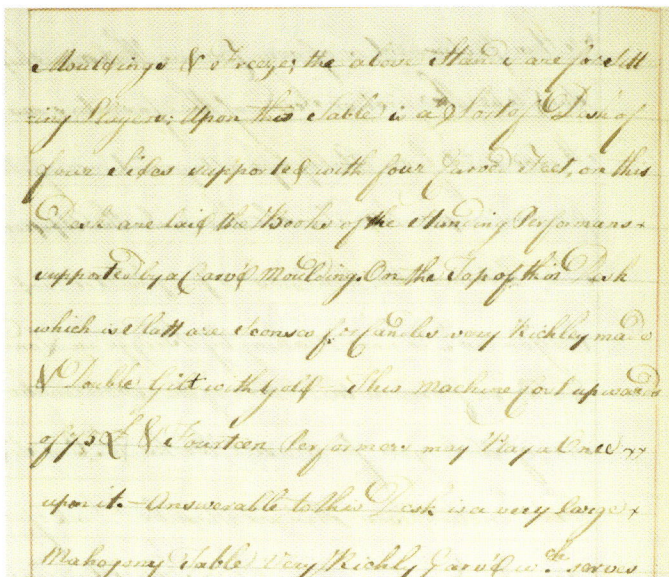

Part of the notes made on a visit to Gopsall Hall in 1750 by John Grundy, the consultant engineer who provided plans for development of the grounds, in which he describes two novelties in Jennens' music room: an instrument which he cannot accurately name but which is clearly a piano (see below) and (on this page) a folding table providing music stands for fourteen players (see p. 47 for transcript).

Jennens' own keyboard instruments. In 1750, as the interiors were being embellished, the consultant engineer John Grundy recorded what he saw there. His account of the music room, 'about 51 Feet long 25 feet wide & 18 feet high', is full of decorative detail:

> The Cornish, Cove & Ceilings of Stucco Adorned with Compartmented Festoons etc & on the four corners of the Ceiling are the Heads of four Eminent Musicians two Foreign & English in Square Frames. The Chimney Piece is of Marble Embellished with musicke instruments on the Frieze.

A frame above the chimney piece was to contain a framed bust of Handel by Roubiliac (one of a number made for Handel's friends). Grundy continues:

> The Furniture of this room is very Grand & Expensive. On each side the Fireplace stands a Harpsicord of one of which is Tabercers? the other made in Italy by a Native of Venice & is called [blank]. Insted of Quill Jacks the strings are struck by small Hammers covered with Leather which makes the tone infinitely softer & more melodious than the Jacks & to prevent the Jar which the too long vibration of the strings occasions there is also small Hammers covered with Leather which falls

George Harris (brother of James Harris, with whom Jennens collaborated on the libretto of *L'Allegro*) records in his diary a dinner on 29 May 1756 at Jennens' London house. The other guests were his brother Thomas Harris, Master in Chancery ('the Master'), Mr Hetherington (Jennens' brother-in-law's clerk and a witness of codicils to Handel's will), and Handel himself, who, 'quite blind, but pretty chearfull', reminisced about his Italian years and played Jennens' piano.

May 29th 56. Dined at Mr. Jennings's, ormond Street. yt Master Handel, Hetherington, — Handel quite Blind, but pretty Chearfull, & after Dinner play'd finely on Mr. J's Piano forte. — Handel Sd, yt Corelli was at yt head of yt orchestra at Rome wn he first went thither; yt 'twas a rule wth Corelli's Band of Music yt wn any one made a Grace, he shd forfeit a Crown; & one poor fidler lost his whole Salary before he cd be cured of Gracing; — Handel was 2 years at Rome in Card. Ottoboni's family. — Handel by birth a Saxon, Wn first He came over to Engld, He played on ye fiddle; but This not Succeeding, He then took to the Harpsichord; —

on the strings to stop in due time the vibration thereof as well as to give due time to each note. This instrument is of very Curious Workmanship. It is said to be the first or second of the Inventor's making. It was sent from Italy by an Acquaintance of Mr Jennens from his travels there.

The instrument that Grundy could not name was one of the first pianos in England, made by the firm of Bartolomeo Cristofori in Florence and despatched by Holdsworth for Jennens from Italy in 1732. Despite having been 'particularly recommended to the care of the captain', it arrived, according to Jennens, rather the worse for its journey, but he apparently subjected it to further excursions, for mutual friends heard Handel play what they described as a pianoforte at Jennens' London house after dinner parties there in 1740 and 1756. Besides the piano and a harpsichord, the music room contained a specially made organ, for which in 1749 Jennens requested, and received (with a cordial note), a specification from Handel.

The final piece of music room furniture which Grundy thought worth noting sheds light on Jennens' music collection.

One side of the Venetian Bow stands a Musick Desk of Mahogany, this Desk is made like a Table standing on four Feet Richly Carved within this Table are Drawers that Draw out on the Sides & Ends in which are Stands for the Books folded up & which are Raised to any height that the Player chooses, the Face of these Drawers are also richly carved as are the Mouldings & Freize, the above Stands are for Sitting Players. Upon this Table is a Sort of Desk of four Sides supported with four Carved Feet, on this Desk are laid the Books of the Standing Performers supported by a carved Moulding. On the top of this Desk which is Flatt are Sconces for Candles very Richly made & Double Gilt with Gold. This Machine cost upwards of 75£ & Fourteen Performers may Play at Once upon it.

The correspondence of Jennens' Harris friends and his cousin Lord Guernsey, an amateur violinist, shows that they all habitually met for domestic chamber music, Jennens included. It seems likely that this music desk with stands for fourteen players was made for such music parties at Gopsall. It could explain the presence of individual part-books, rather than just scores, among the manuscripts in Jennens' Handel collection. It enlarges our understanding of his figuring of the bass lines (inserting suggested harmonisations) in copies of Handel's works that were made for him. A local tradition has it that Handel's *Jephtha* was tried out at Gopsall before its London premiere in 1752, to which the furnishing of the music room gives some credence. It is pleasant to think of the often lonely Jennens making music with his friends.

6

*'Mr Handel has his fits of hard labour
as well as of idleness'*

WORKING WITH HANDEL

❧

THREE MAJOR commitments informed Jennens' life: his
devotion to Handel's music, his Christian faith, and his
political loyalties. They also fuelled his libretto writing.

Jennens subscribed to the prevailing eighteenth-century
view that good art improves its recipients, and that those who
are able to create good art have an obligation to do so, to the
highest standards. Fostering artists' potential was a theme of
his own life, whether commissioning buildings, interior decoration, paintings and sculpture, or subscribing to composers'
performances and publications, or persuading and helping
Holdsworth to complete and publish his Virgil research.
Writing librettos for Handel was the most proactive of his
engagements with the arts. Whereas others who provided texts
for Handel, such as Humphreys and Morell, were approached
by the composer with the request for a libretto, Jennens more
often got Handel to write in response to his ideas, and on occa-
sion to rewrite as well.

In July 1733 Jennens revisited Oxford for the university
degree ceremonies (Encaenia), at which his young cousin Lord
Guernsey gave one of the undergraduate orations, and Handel
provided several concerts. The major musical event was the first
performance of Handel's third English oratorio, *Athalia* –
containing music based on the manuscripts of operas by
Alessandro Scarlatti which Jennens had loaned Handel from

Handel by Thomas
Hudson, painted three
years before his death,
in 1756, with the score
of *Messiah* open in
front of him: this
'Gopsall' portrait,
commissioned by
Jennens, is the largest
known painting of the
composer (239 x 146
cm). The magnificent
frame, with trophies of
musical instruments
and scores, is the orig-
inal one and may be
the work of the French
Catholic Joseph
Duffour, a leading
London carver and
gilder and a supplier of
ornament in papier
mâché, whom
Handel's friend Mrs
Delany called 'the
famous man for paper
ornaments like stucco'.

his collection. Hearing *Athalia* in Oxford and at its London revival in 1735 was perhaps what prompted Jennens to write an (unidentified) oratorio libretto and send it to Handel, the earliest evidence we have of his broaching collaboration with the composer. Handel's grateful acknowledgment (July 1735) indicates that Jennens had suggested he include a new oratorio in his next season, something which he had not done in London since 1733. When Handel did again programme a new oratorio, in 1739, the text was by Jennens: *Saul*.

Fostering Handel's art

Handel was the only composer for whom Jennens wrote. It was not a vanity exercise. His librettos were all anonymous. It was not for gain. Unlike other writers, he made Handel a present of his librettos (as Handel acknowledged in the only surviving correspondence between them about their collaboration). It was at least partly in order to further Handel's success. The genesis of *L'Allegro, il Penseroso ed il Moderato* is a striking example.

When in late 1739 Handel set aside the libretto for *Messiah* which Jennens had given him, Jennens acted on Handel's remark that in the coming season he wanted 'to please the town with something of a gayer turn'. He urged their mutual friend James Harris to implement his idea of a libretto based on Milton's two contrasting character studies of the extrovert and the reflective person, *L'Allegro* and *Il Penseroso*. He then pushed the project through at a speed entirely foreign to the deliberate, thoughtful pace that was natural to him, in order to fit Handel's timetable. He was aiming to ensure that Handel produced *good* work, writing to Harris 'by all means let me know your intentions by the next post, for he is so eager that I am afraid, if his demands are not answer'd very soon, he will be diverted to some less agreeable design'. In working on Harris' enthusiasm, Jennens would have been aware that Milton was good material for Handel's career. Milton was enjoying what amounted to cult esteem as the most revered British author of all time. Moreover, in the previous year Handel's only rival for supremacy in serious English theatre music, Thomas Augustine Arne, had had a huge success with a setting of Milton's *Comus*. *L'Allegro* would enable Handel to stake his own claim to the greatest English poet. Similarly, in the following year, mindful of Handel's depleted finances, Jennens hoped that *Messiah* could be performed as a benefit concert for him (Handel taking the box office profits, as at his benefit 'Oratorio' in 1738), during the week before Easter, when the spoken theatres would be dark, potentially increasing Handel's audience.

The collaboration of librettist and composer seems sometimes to have involved face-to-face discussion, but usually only when the libretto was fairly well advanced. The works for which we have the fullest testimony are *L'Allegro* and *Belshazzar*. For *L'Allegro* Jennens was initially a conduit between Harris and Handel, taking decisions when time precluded extensive consultation. *Belshazzar* was immensely problematic, in that Jennens' pace was far slower than suited Handel. The librettist sent the composer each act at an interval of nearly a month; Handel had to ask twice for Act 3, and when it came he responded plaintively: 'you may believe that I think it a very fine and sublime Oratorio, only it is realy too long, if I should extend the Musick, it would last 4 Hours and more'. Jennens grumbled to Holdsworth, but seems to have made no fuss to Handel about the loss of 288 of his 797 lines.

Handel enthusiasts of the last two centuries have often condemned Jennens for presuming to critique the composer. His manner to Handel (and Handel's to him), despite their relative ages (Jennens was fifteen years Handel's junior), was partly the result of their respective social positions and the conventions of their time. But his touchiness about Handel's work was not mere pique or pride. It was at least equally due to a desire for Handel always to do justice to *himself*, to his own gifts and potential (as in the remark made during the composition of *L'Allegro* that heads this chapter).

Jennens could have complained, but never did, that he put an enormous amount of research, thought and effort into his librettos, incidentally giving the lie to the mantra of his day that libretto writing was a mere bagatelle. For *Belshazzar*, for example, he drew on the Bible (Isaiah, Jeremiah, Ezra, Psalms, Daniel), ancient history (Josephus, Herodotus, Xenophon, Polybius), and contemporary political ideology (Charles Rollin's *Ancient History*, Andrew Ramsay's *The Travels of Cyrus*, Lord Bolingbroke's *The Idea of a Patriot King*). For *Saul* he condensed into 510 lines a narrative stretching over twenty-six chapters of the Bible, material from the Psalms, and whole scenes derived from non-biblical sources. In his rendition of David's elegy for Saul and Jonathan, an eighteenth-century testing ground for the esteemed art of poetic paraphrase, the rhyme scheme and stress pattern are the same only in the first and last of the nine stanzas; yet alongside the demands imposed by this structural display, with one exception Jennens retains the sequence of ideas of the original and surpasses all other contemporary paraphrases for accuracy – a remarkable feat which, as he would have anticipated, is mostly masked in the musical setting.

Where Jennens felt that Handel had misinterpreted his intentions he sometimes amended the copies of finished scores that were made for him, most famously placing consistent stress on 'stand' in 'I know that my redeemer liveth' in *Messiah*, turning Handel's elegant variation into an unwavering statement of faith. This is an index both of what he really cared about and of how much he cared, for his changes seem to have been made only for his own domestic use. A comment to Holdsworth about *Messiah* shows his principal concern to have been that Handel respect the importance of the subject:

> he has made a fine Entertainment of it, tho' not near so good as he might & ought to have done. I have with great difficulty made him correct some of the grossest faults in the composition, but he retain'd his Overture obstinately, in which there are some passages far unworthy of Handel, but much more unworthy of the Messiah.

As Jennens says, Handel attended to his comments, and not only for *Messiah*. He successfully, and aptly, persuaded Handel not to add a Hallelujah to the end of *Saul*, which concludes with an expectation of continuing struggle, but to set the (appropriate) Hallelujah at the opening, which the composer had initially rejected. Handel adopted his suggestion to use two of the Cannons anthems in *Belshazzar*. Handel accepted his opinion that Milton's 'At a solemn musick' would not make a good tailpiece to *L'Allegro* and *Il Penseroso*, with which it would indeed have sat most oddly, finishing a genial secular entertainment with an ecstatic religious rhapsody; instead Handel let him write 'A little piece [actually the longest wholly original

Overleaf: Pages from the original (1739) wordbook of Jennens' *Saul*, Part 3: the elegy for Saul and Jonathan. The story of Saul's overthrow was linked in the public mind with the execution of Charles I, whose image Jennens chose for his seal. The assassination of Saul and David's lament for Saul and Jonathan (II Samuel 1) formed the Old Testament reading at the penitential service held annually throughout Britain on the anniversary of Charles I's execution. David's lament, carefully paraphrased and versified by Jennens, is the extended climax of the intense final part of *Saul* and inspired one of Handel's most moving compositional sequences.

SCENE V.

ELEGY on the Death of SAUL and JONATHAN.

I.

MOURN, Israel, *mourn, thy Beauty lost,*
 Thy choicest Youth on Gilboa *slain.*
How have thy fairest Hopes been crost !
 What Heaps of mighty Warriors strow the Plain !

II.

 O let it not in Gath *be heard,*
The News in Askelon *let none proclaim ;*
 Lest we, whom once so much they fear'd,
  Be by their Women now despis'd,
  And lest the Daughters of th' Uncircumcis'd
Rejoice and triumph in our Shame.

III.

  From this unhappy Day,
 No more, ye Gilboan *Hills, on you*
Descend refreshing Rain or kindly Dew,
  Which erst your Heads with Plenty crown'd ;
  Since there the Shield of Saul, *in Arms renown'd,*
  Was vilely cast away.

IV.

 Brave Jonathan *his Bow ne'er drew,*
 But wing'd with Death his Arrow flew,
And drank the Blood of slaughter'd Foes :
 Nor drew Great Saul *his Sword in vain ;*
It reek'd, where'er he dealt his Blows,
 With Entrails of the mighty Slain.

V. Eagles

V.

Eagles were not so swift as they,
Nor Lions with so strong a Grasp held fast and tore the Prey.

VI.

In sweetest Harmony they liv'd,
Nor Death their Union cou'd divide :
The pious Son ne'er left his Father's Side,
But him defending bravely dy'd :
A Loss too great to be surviv'd !

VII.

For Saul, ye Maids of Israel, moan,
To whose indulgent Care
You owe the Scarlet and the Gold you wear,
And all the Pomp in which your Beauty long has shone.

VIII.

O fatal Day ! How low the Mighty lie !
O Jonathan ! how nobly didst thou die,
For thy King and Country slain !
For thee, my Brother Jonathan,
How great is my Distress !
What Language can my Grief express ?
Great was the Pleasure I enjoy'd in thee !
And more than Woman's Love thy wondrous Love to me !

IX.

O fatal Day ! How low the Mighty lie !
Where, Israel, is thy Glory fled ?
Spoil'd of thy Arms, and sunk in Infamy,
How canst thou raise again thy drooping Head !

ABIATHAR.

An early manuscript score (1740) of Handel's *L'Allegro, il Penseroso ed il Moderato* owned and annotated by Jennens. Here, in part of the climactic duet of *Il Moderato*, 'As steals the morn' (with words adapted by Jennens from Shakespeare's *The Tempest*), he has inserted the marking 'pianiss[imo]' and, as in many of the scores made for him, he has figured the bass line, indicating an intention to play as well as to own.

English text written for Handel to set]… to which He gave the Name of Il Moderato, & which united those two independent Poems in one Moral Design'. Handel lent Jennens his autograph scores and allowed him to annotate them with suggested amendments, some of which he accommodated – a mark of respect for his collaborator's judgment which he seems not to have accorded to any other librettist. But in the case of *Messiah*, Jennens was under few illusions: Handel was willing to make alterations because he wanted Jennens to write him another libretto:

> Handel has promis'd to revise the Oratorio of Messiah, & He & I are very good Friends again. The reason is, he has lately lost his Poet Miller [by death], & wants to set me at work for him again. Religion & Morality, Gratitude, Good Nature & Good Sense had been better Principles of Action than this Single Point of Interest but I must take him as I find him and make the best use I can of him (7 May 1744).

One way of making best use of Handel was to write to his

Subscribing himself 'your most affectionate Friend', Jennens confides to Holdsworth his feelings about the resumption of his collaboration with Handel after their falling-out over *Messiah* (transcript opposite).

strengths and extend them, and this Jennens did with more flair than any other of Handel's English librettists.

Writing for Handel

Messiah reveals Jennens' understanding of Handel's needs. On the face of it, a complex, meditative, doctrinal text about revelation and salvation was unsuited to a gestural dramatic composer whose compositional method was to proceed by structured contrasts. But *Messiah* is a powerfully affecting work for millions of listeners in part because Jennens responded to Handel's style. So that Handel could deploy the full range of his dramatising ability, Jennens interleaved occasional thumbnail scenes, such as the annunciation to the shepherds, or the mocking of Christ. More pervasively, the text is shot through with the concrete imagery of the Old Testament, giving Handel the cues for vivid evocation that he needed, such as a straight highway in the desert, a potter's vessel being smashed, a refiner's fire. Jennens skilfully pruned his texts of competing and lesser images in the same biblical verse, for example removing the fuller's soap from 'for he is like a refiner's fire, and like fuller's soap...'. Suggestive and arresting, the images enabled Handel to convey ideas in the manner of a preacher using a homely analogy, more readily than through an abstract conceptual text.

Yet more boldly, Jennens used Old Testament text to convey the Christian message of redemption, so that the account of Christ's sacrifice could be expressed by Handel through illustration (such as the lashes of the smiters). Moreover, in choosing to depict the Passion with the traditional texts from Isaiah, Jennens afforded scope to another of Handel's unique gifts: his power to evoke the pathos of the suffering human being.

Jennens was alive to Handel's contrast system, whether in major transitions, such as the shift in perspective from God's universal rule at the end of Part 2 to God's attention to the individual believer at the start of Part 3, or in contrasts within sections, such as darkness and light (a Handel favourite) in Part 1. Here the duplication of the dark–light image allowed Handel to show the variety of his invention, the first contrast being expressed in melodic, the second in harmonic terms. Jennens' choice of texts elicited from Handel an epitome of oratorio's power to be at once drama and meditation.

The unprecedented form of *Messiah* – no named characters, no overall narrative, short passages of text, minimal recitative – likewise served to draw new qualities of expressiveness from Handel. Jennens made formal innovations in every libretto he compiled. *Israel in Egypt*, which may be his compilation, or on which he may have assisted, was a wholly novel choral epic, a forerunner of *Messiah* in using only Scripture, verbatim. *Saul* and *Belshazzar* moved English oratorio to new planes of dramatic and psychological realism.

For *Saul* Jennens gave Handel, and oratorio, a new form of interaction between characters. In the first soloists' scene there are more characters with substantive solo parts in one scene than in any music theatre work yet heard in Britain – seven, of

M E S S I A H,

A N

O R A T O R I O.

Set to Mufick by GEORGE-FREDERIC HANDEL, Efq;.

M A J O R A   C A N A M U S.

*And without Controverfy, great is the Myftery of Godli-
nefs : God was manifefted in the Flefh, juftify'd by the Spirit,
feen of Angels, preached among the Gentiles, believed on in
the World, received up in Glory.*

*In whom are hid all the Treafures of Wifdom and Know-
ledge.*

L O N D O N:

Printed and Sold by THO. WOOD in *Windmill-Court*, near *Weft-
Smithfield*, and at the THEATRE in *Covent-Garden*. 1743.

[Price One Shilling.]

A facsimile of the title page of the wordbook for the first London performances of *Messiah*. Jennens had sent Handel its epigraphs for the first performances in Dublin. One of the epigraphs both announces the stature of the work's theme and universalises it: 'Majora canamus' (we sing of greater things), from Virgil's Fourth Eclogue, invokes the 18th-century belief that the revered classical pagan authors acknowledged the Messiah. The biblical texts (I Timothy 3.16; Colossians 2.3) encapsulate Jennens' high Anglican creed and the groundplan of his libretto, insisting that Christianity does not depend on reason and need have no recourse to rational argument, for revelation *is* a mystery. Unlike the Dublin libretto, this printing – which divides each of the three parts of the text into distinct subsections – is thought to have Jennens' authority.

whom six are actual or incipient family relations. Here Jennens implanted his love of Shakespeare into Handelian drama, moving oratorio away from the manner of opera seria, in which conversations are between only two or three people. At the same time Jennens transformed the theocentric biblical epic into a drama of feeling, akin to the many plays of the contemporary stage which celebrated warm and refined sensibility. Into a history concerned mainly with obedience to God as God, Jennens injected humanitarian ideas about moral goodness, friendship and generosity. *Saul* embodies a clear moral scheme in the contrasted characters of the virtuous, devout David and the tyrannical, apostate Saul.

Jennens, writing *Belshazzar*, has left a letter from Holdsworth unanswered for four months and grumbles to him (26 September 1744) that it is Handel's fault: 'my Muse is such a Jade, & Handel hurry'd her so, that I could not find time for writing Letters.' But he wrote *Belshazzar* not only to oblige Handel: 'the truth is, I had a farther view in it'.

A similar antithesis, between Cyrus and Belshazzar, underpins the epic events of *Belshazzar*, in which Jennens specified a chorus representing by turns three distinct nations (not the usual oratorio one or two), so that Handel could (and did) give characterising musical qualities to each. In *Belshazzar* we literally see Jennens' appreciation of Handel's need to imagine dramatic action. Handel wrote oratorio as opera of the mind, not for acted stage performance. But Jennens knew that Handel, a consummate man of the theatre, would write at his best if he was able to visualise the drama while he composed it. So he wrote scene settings and 'stage directions' into the text that he gave to Handel (and to the printer of the wordbooks which the audience would follow during the performance); and Handel copied them into his working score. The 'stage directions' for Belshazzar's Feast are particularly vivid, and famously inspired Handel:

> As he is going to drink, a Hand appears writing upon the Wall over-against him; he sees it, turns pale with Fear, drops the Bowl of Wine, falls back in his Seat, trembling from Head to Foot, and his Knees knocking against each other.

Jennens made 'best use' of Handel by writing to, and

extending, his abilities. But his comment 'I must take him as I find him, & make the best use I can of him', and his remark to Holdsworth after he had written *Belshazzar*, 'the truth is, I had a farther view in it' (26 September 1744), indicate a personal investment in writing for Handel. Reading his librettos in the light of contemporary events and ideas, we can discern that Jennens was 'using' the composer as a conduit for his own values: for his deeply held Christian beliefs and his political loyalties.

Making use of Handel

Like others of conservative Christian persuasion, especially those non-jurors committed to the mystical interpretation of doctrine, Jennens deplored the inroads that science, scholarship and rationalism were making on faith. For Protestants the Bible was the bedrock of life, and of life after death. Most Britons had until recently believed that God rewarded virtue and punished sin in the eternal life to come, in which hell fire could be avoided only through the intercession of the divine redeemer: the Messiah prophesied in the Old Testament and hailed in the gospels. But the new scientific and Enlightenment rationalism called the integrity of the Bible and the truth of revelation into question (see chapter 2).

The evangelically minded Jennens had the genius to see that the people most alienated from Christianity, and hence most

Jennens' hopes for *Messiah*: in a letter to Holdsworth of 10 July 1741, among much other news, Jennens mentions a libretto he has compiled for Handel: 'Handel says he will do nothing next Winter, but I hope I shall perswade him to set another Scripture Collection I have made for him, & perform it for his own Benefit in Passion week. I hope he will lay out his whole Genius & Skill upon it, that the Composition may excell all his former Compositions, as the Subject excells every other Subject. The Subject is Messiah.'

in danger of eternal damnation, were the least likely to be reached by sermons and tracts, but could be reached by the emotional power of Handel's music. In the week before Easter such people would be more likely to attend a theatre than a church, if they could, but no plays, no operas, no pantomimes were allowed. But oratorios were allowed, because of their religious content; and Handel performed his oratorios in a theatre. So Jennens conceived *Messiah* for Passion week, so that those most in need of being reminded of their duty to their faith, the theatre audience, would – perhaps taken unawares – hear its message, and be moved to prepare themselves properly for the holiest days of the year. For them the choice of texts would have had particular point. *Messiah* is an epitome of Christian doctrine as expressed in the Apostles' creed (recited in the Anglican morning and evening services). Nearly all the texts in *Messiah* are also in the liturgy of the major feasts of the Christian year. Jennens chose texts that would remind Handel's audience of their religious identity, texts whose resonances were second nature to them, because they had heard them, year in, year out, in their childhood if not since. Besides reaffirming the faith of the faithful, *Messiah* was a summons to those who knew what they should believe, but were in danger of forgetting. Enlightenment rationalism questioned whether the Newtonian ruler of the cosmos could be interested in the fate of every human being. *Messiah* responded affirmatively with a reminder of personal judgment, redemption and eternal life.

Jennens was the only defender of Christianity to conceive the benefits of harnessing Handel's emotive force to the message of redemption. But original as *Messiah* was, to Jennens it would not have been peculiar in Handel's output. He knew that Handel had already written about Jesus Christ as saviour in Italian in the Roman Catholic tradition (*La Resurrezione*, 1708) and in German in the Lutheran tradition (the *Brockes Passion*, 1716). To him it could have been obvious that there was a gap for Handel to fill: in English in the Anglican tradition. He could also have identified *Israel in Egypt* as a precursor, whether or not he was involved in its creation, for it too conveys the message of divine miraculous salvation with biblical texts.

When Jennens was at his most distressed by what Handel had made of his *Messiah* libretto, he told Holdsworth: 'I will put no more sacred words into his hands, to be thus abus'd.' But two years later, in *Belshazzar*, Jennens drew on twenty-one chapters of Bible, quoted it repeatedly, and twice even brought the Scriptures 'onstage' (when Daniel reads them to his fellow Jews, and when he shows them to Prince Cyrus).

Messiah reaffirms time-honoured 'evidence' of Christianity, the Old Testament prophecies of the Messiah which were seen to be fulfilled in the New Testament. *Belshazzar* contains an even more determined defence of Old Testament prophecies. The prophecies that Jennens quotes in this libretto do not explicitly predict the Messiah. Instead, they are the prophecies in Isaiah which name Prince Cyrus and foretell his conquest of Babylon, his liberation of the Jews held captive there, his restoration of them to Jerusalem, and his decree for the rebuilding of their temple there – all of which actually happened. With this more modest but more conclusive demonstration of the reliability of scriptural prophecy about a redeemer, Jennens cleverly implies that prophecy so triumphantly fulfilled in one instance can be trusted everywhere. Moreover, the prophecies of Cyrus by Isaiah occur in the very same chapters as the prophecies customarily interpreted as foretelling the coming of the Messiah. In Christian cultures Cyrus was traditionally given symbolic significance as a foreshadowing of the Messiah. Jennens was saying: Isaiah was right about Cyrus; so how can you doubt that he was right about the Messiah too. In addition, Jennens' central source is the Book of Daniel, which contains the first explicit reference in the Bible to resurrection and the last judgement (12:2). To ratify Daniel – as Jennens' text does ceaselessly – is to ratify the promise of resurrection.

Throughout *Belshazzar* Jennens dovetailed the Bible's

Overleaf: Pages from the wordbook of *Belshazzar* issued for the 1751 revival, showing Jennens' careful and pointed references to his sources: the prophecies of Cyrus' redemption of the Jews in the biblical books of Isaiah and Jeremiah are ratified by the Greek historian Xenophon. (The vertical lines show text omitted in performance.)

That I proceed in nothing with Neglect *
Of Pow'r divine: Whate'er I undertake,
I still begin with God, and gain his Favour
By Sacrifice and Prayer.

CHORUS.

All Empires upon God depend;
Begun by his Command, at his Command they end.
Look up to him in all your Ways:
Begin with Pray'r, and end with Praise.
- - - - - *Without his Aid you war in vain:*
- - - - - *Be subject: —— 'Tis the way to reign.*

S C E N E III.

DANIEL's House.

Daniel, *with the Prophecies of* Isaiah *and* Jeremiah *open before him: Other* Jews.

A I R.

Dan.   *O sacred Oracles of Truth!*
          O living Spring of purest Joy!
          By Day be ever in my Mouth,
          And all my nightly Thoughts employ.
          Whoe'er withhold Attention due
          Neglect themselves, despising you.   Da Capo.

RECIT. *accompany'd.*

Rejoice, my Countrymen: The Time draws near,
The long expected Time herein foretold.   *Jer.* xxix.
Seek now the Lord your God with all your Heart,
And you shall surely find him.   He shall turn
Your long Captivity: he shall gather you
From all the Nations whither you are driven,
And to your native Land in Peace restore you.

          O Lord! the great and dreadful God!
          Justly thou hast thy Curses pour'd
              On our rebellious Heads:
          For ours and for our Fathers Sins
          Thy People are become the Scorn
              Of all the Nations round.

                                                                        Yet

* Xenoph. Cyrop. lib. 1.

Yet in thy Wrath remember Mercy :
O ! be thy Fury turn'd away :
   Not for our Righteoufnefs,
But for thine own great Mercies fake !
  O Lord, hear : O Lord, forgive :
Defer not, for thine own fake, O our God ! ——
  For we are thine, and bear thy Name.

Dan. Doubt not, our Pray'r is heard; ——
For long ago,
Whole Ages ere this *Cyrus* yet was born
Or thought of, Great *Jehovah*, by his Prophet,
In Words of Comfort to his captive People
Foretold, and call'd by Name the wondrous Man.

R e c i t. *accompany'd.*

" Thus faith the Lord to *Cyrus* his Anointed,   *Ifa.* xliv. & xlv.
" Whofe right Hand I have holden, to fubdue
" Nations before him : I will go before thee,
" To loofe the Strong-knit Loins of mighty Kings,
" Make ftraight the crooked Places, break in pieces
" The Gates of folid Brafs, and cut in funder
" The Bars of Iron. For my Servants fake,
" *Ifr'el* my Chofen, though thou haft not known me,
" I have furnam'd thee: I have girded thee :
" That from the rifing to the fetting Sun
" The Nations may confefs, I am the Lord,
" There is none elfe, there is no God befides me.
" Thou fhalt perform my Pleafure, to *Jerufalem*
" Saying, Thou fhalt be built; and to the Temple,
" Thy raz'd Foundation fhall again be laid."

CHORUS.

Sing, O ye Heavens, for the Lord hath done it :
  Earth, from thy Center fhout :
Break forth, ye Mountains, into Songs of Joy,
  O Foreft, and each Tree therein :
Jehovah hath redeemed Jacob,
And glorify'd himfelf in Ifrael.   Hallelujah.

account of the fall of Babylon with the account given by the ancient Greek historians, showing how exactly they match, and proving it in his libretto with textual references. His message to Handel's audience was that pagan, non-Christian authors, who had no religious agenda, nevertheless provided a narrative that replicates the Bible, to an amazing degree of detail; so even for those who lack faith, it is only reasonable to believe the Bible.

There is also a great deal in *Belshazzar* to engage an audience which is entirely secular in outlook. *Belshazzar* reflects on kingship, empire, freedom and war. Prince Cyrus as described by Xenophon in his *Cyropaedia* was a favourite eighteenth-century model of the Patriot King: a magnanimous, modest, unostentatious, law-giving, law-abiding and religious leader, who conquered to bring peace and to free the oppressed, who was a loyal personal friend as well as a far-seeing empire builder, who won hearts by his generous personal touch and who set an example of devout obedience to divine will. This was the prescription of a good ruler in eighteenth-century British political tracts, and it is the character of Cyrus in *Belshazzar*.

Belshazzar's politics also encompass a more partisan view – Jennens' own. For those who shared his political sympathies, the exiled and finally restored Jews in *Belshazzar* would readily have been understood as the exiled Stuart kings of Britain and their supporters, and as those at home, Jennens among them, suffering a form of internal exile. The end of *Belshazzar* envisages a peaceful restoration in which all opposing factions will be reconciled. Like so much opposition writing of all periods it is idealistic and visionary. But alongside its wishful thinking, the libretto of *Belshazzar* has a political maturity unique among Handel's biblical dramas. Although Britain was fighting an international imperialist war while it was being written, there is no triumphalism, nationalism, or vengeance; the hero's aim is bloodless conquest, peace, liberty and good government; goodness is not the preserve of a single nation or race; generous, courageous, wise people of three different nations collaborate for the benefit of others; at the end all the participants except a wicked tyrant are honourably treated, safe and free.

Saul is similarly imbued with Jennens' own political outlook, and more explicitly refers to his own dilemma. The biblical story tells of the replacement of the divinely appointed but increasingly lawless Saul with the non-royal but godly David. In the vast amount of British debate about the lawfulness of the changes of rulership from Stuarts to Hanoverians, both sides constantly invoked the story of Saul and David to bolster their arguments. The story was even built into the fabric of the state religion. Each year, on the anniversary of Charles I's execution, a penitential service was held in churches throughout the country, and in Parliament, to expiate the communal crime of killing the Lord's anointed. The reading from the Old Testament in this commemorative service was David's Lament for Saul and Jonathan – the text which forms the basis of the great extended climax of *Saul*.

For Jennens, ideologically committed to the cause of Charles I's descendants, the death of Saul had special, complicated resonance. The killing of Saul, the anointed king, was (like the killing of Charles I) terrible sacrilege. But equally, Jennens inscribed his libretto with his anguished acknowledgment that the lawless, apostate Saul had to be set aside, just as the rightful but Catholic king James II had had to be set aside because of his backsliding from what Jennens, a devout Church of England Protestant, held to be the true religion. That painful sense of irreconcilable claims gave Handel material with which to raise Saul's final scene to a level of personal tragedy unique in his oratorios.

The collaboration of Handel and Jennens was between two forthright, determined men whose agendas were often at variance. Handel found other librettists far more tractable. But Jennens brought him a passionate concern to make good art and convey worthwhile messages; a nuanced political awareness; a mind well stocked with literature and learning; a keen

appreciation of Handel's gifts and needs; and – often over-looked – flexibility and versatility. When Handel wanted something other than *Messiah*, Jennens quickly surrendered divine mystery for secular entertainment. Nor did he let the 'concept' of *L'Allegro*'s libretto be confused by a religious text which must have appealed greatly to him. Having rejected 'At a Solemn Musick', he could nevertheless have infused his own concluding text for *L'Allegro* with a Christian version of stoicism. But, in sympathy with his fellow librettist's philosophy and the tenor of the rest of the work, he finished *Il Moderato* with a hymn to 'intellectual day' illuminated by the light of reason. His flexibility, however, did not extend to denying his principles, however privately held. Handel apparently knew him well enough not to ask him for oratorio librettos celebrating the defeat of the Jacobite rebellion of 1745.

[21]

SCENE IV.

DAVID, *&c.* *To them an* Amalekite.

David. Whence comeſt thou ?
Amal. Out of the Camp of *Ifrael.*
David. Thou canſt inform me then : How went the Battle ?
Amal. The People, put to flight, in Numbers fell,
 And *Saul,* and *Jonathan* his Son, are dead.
David. Alas ! my Brother ! —— But how know'ſt thou
 That they are dead ?
Amal. Upon Mount *Gilboa*
 I met with *Saul,* juſt fall'n upon his Spear.
 Swiftly the Foe purſu'd. He cry'd to me,
 Begg'd me to finiſh his imperfect Work,
 And end a Life of Pain and Ignominy.
 I knew he could not live, and therefore flew him ;
 Took from his Head the Crown, and from his Arms
 The Bracelets, and have brought them to my Lord.
David. Whence art thou ?
Amal. I am an *Amalekite.*

DAVID.

Impious Wretch, of Race accurſt !
And of all that Race the worſt !
How haſt thou dar'd to lift thy Sword
Againſt th' Anointed of the Lord ?
Fall on him —— ſmite him —— let him die ;   [To one of his At-
On thy own Head thy Blood will lie ;   tendants, who kills
Since thy own Mouth has teſtify'd,   the *Amalekite.*
By Thee the Lord's Anointed dy'd.

SCENE

Jennens' wordbook of *Saul*, Part 3: the death of Saul. For Jennens, and for many of his contemporaries, the killing of King Saul symbolised the execution of the Stuart King Charles I, and he transcribed his appalled horror at the regicide into his libretto.

Opposite: Part of the same scene in Handel's autograph score of *Saul*, which he had loaned to Jennens: the start of David's air 'Impious wretch', amended by Jennens to bring the voice in directly after the preceding recitative and before the ritornello, expressing outrage at the killing of 'the Lord's Anointed'. The words 'Impious wretch' and the three notes in the first bar of the vocal line (stave 3) are in Jennens' hand.

And from 1747 Jennens' role as squire of Gopsall and inheritor of extensive properties (see chapter 4) provided a new channel for his creative energy. But the friendship of librettist and composer continued to the end of Handel's life, and was perhaps the more amiable when freed from the pressures of collaboration.

'A man of great piety, beneficence, and taste in the Fine Arts'

FINIS

Despite his hypochondria Jennens lived into his seventies, an advanced age in the eighteenth century. His innovative contributions to the arts continued to his final years, culminating in his Shakespeare editions. Age and infirmity did not dim his intellectual energy or his desire to be productive.

The candid account of Jennens' character, in the funeral sermon by his local vicar (and fellow Balliol alumnus), the Rev. George Kelly, ends with a vivid account of his death:

> ... there might appear in him a Degree of Shyness, and a reserved Disposition, especially in mixt Companies, which some might construe into a Moroseness and Singularity of Temper. But they who had better Opportunities of his Acquaintance well knew to the contrary; and can with much Truth say, that few could be more unreserved and open in Conversation than he whenever he was able to throw off that Depression of Spirits, which seemed natural to him. In short, it was the Observation of some particular Friends, that he was remarkably alert the Night before his Departure, which then gave us reason to hope that Providence would have extended so valuable a Life to a later Period. But how were we disappointed! For within a few Hours after he was snatched away from us in the most sudden and unexpected Manner; not however insensible of his fast approaching End, and requesting the last Prayers of his Chaplain, Part of which Office being performed, he threw himself back into his Chair, and instantly expired. The unalterable Summons he chearfully obeyed; and in the Words of holy Simeon seemed to say, Lord, now lettest thou thy Servant depart in Peace according to thy Word.

Above: Jennens' burial monument, Nether Whitacre church; *Below:* Holdsworth's cenotaph, commissioned by Jennens, which stood at Gopsall under the temple surmounted by Roubiliac's statute of Religion. Both are by Richard Hayward. Both show a crumbling pyramid through which leafy branches are pushing, symbolising the promise of life after death. Jennens' monument is inscribed 'Non omnis moriar' (Horace Odes III.xxx.6), 'I will not entirely die'. The pyramid on Holdsworth's monument additionally pays tribute to his reputation as the country's leading Virgil scholar, being copied from a contemporary illustration of the monument believed to be Virgil's tomb (near Naples, and visited by Holdsworth on his Italian travels), on which the greenery was famously self-renewing.

SELECT BIBLIOGRAPHY AND FURTHER READING

The two main sources for Jennens' biography are his correspondence with his friend Edward Holdsworth, 1729–46 (Gerald Coke Handel Collection, The Foundling Museum), and the account in Nichols' *Leicester* (see below). The papers of the Harris family (Hampshire Record Office: see Burrows and Dunhill below) contain important letters relating to Jennens' collaboration with Handel. Jennens' surviving correspondence with Handel is scattered; it has been published in *Händel Handbuch* (see below) and will appear in *Handel Documents* (Cambridge University Press, 2013–14). The Royal Institute of British Architects Library contains 89 drawings for Gopsall. Further sources are given in Smith, 'The Achievements' (see below).

Bindman, David, and Malcolm Baker: *Roubiliac and the Eighteenth-Century Monument* (New Haven and London, 1995)

Burrows, Donald: *Handel: Messiah* (Cambridge, 1991)

Burrows, Donald: 'Handel and the Pianoforte', *Göttinger Händel Beiträge* 9 (2002), 123–41

Burrows, Donald: *Handel* (Master Musicians series), 2nd edn (Oxford, 2012)

Burrows, Donald, ed.: *The Cambridge Companion to Handel* (Cambridge, 1997)

Burrows, Donald, and Rosemary Dunhill, eds: *Music and Theatre in Handel's World: The Family Papers of James Harris, 1732–1780* (Oxford, 2002)

Dean, Winton: *Handel's Dramatic Oratorios and Masques* (London, 1959)

Eisen, Walter and Margret: *Händel Handbuch*, vol. 4, *Dokumente zu Leben und Schaffen* (Leipzig, 1985)

Everett, Paul J.: 'A Roman Concerto Repertory: Ottoboni's "WhatNot"?', *Proceedings of the Royal Musical Association* 110 (1983–84), 62–78

Ferdinand, Christine: *An Accidental Masterpiece: Magdalen College's New Building and the People who Built It* (Oxford, 2010)

Friedman, T. F.: 'Gopsall Hall', *Catalogue of the Drawings Collection of the RIBA, G-K* (London, 1973), pp. 130–2

Gudger, William: 'George Frideric Handel's 1749 Letter to Charles Jennens' in *The Rosaleen Moldenhauer Memorial: Music History from Primary Sources – A Guide to the Moldenhauer Archives*, ed. Jon Newsom and Alfred Mann (Washington, DC, 2000)

Hicks, Anthony: 'Handel, Jennens and *Saul*: Aspects of a Collaboration', in *Music and Theatre: Essays in honour of Winton Dean*, ed. Nigel Fortune (Cambridge, 1987), pp. 203–27

Jones, John: *Balliol College: A History 1263–1939* (Oxford, 1988)

Nichols, John: *The History and Antiquities of the County of Leicester*, IV/2 (London, 1811, facsimile reprint East Ardsley, 1971), pp. 856–9

Overton, J. H.: *The Nonjurors* (London, 1902)

Roberts, John H.: 'Handel and Charles Jennens's Italian Opera Manuscripts', in *Music and Theatre: Essays in honour of Winton Dean*, ed. Nigel Fortune (Cambridge, 1987), pp. 159–201

Roberts, John H.: 'The Aylesford Collection', in *Handel Collections and their History*, ed. Terence Best (Oxford, 1993), pp. 39–85

Smith, Ruth: 'The Achievements of Charles Jennens', *Music and Letters* 70 (1989), 161–90

Smith, Ruth: *Handel's Oratorios and Eighteenth-Century Thought* (Cambridge, 1995)

Sumner, Brenda: 'Charles Jennens' Piano and Music Room', *Handel Institute Newsletter* 22/2 (Autumn 2011)

Talbot, Michael: 'Charles Jennens and Antonio Vivaldi' in *Vivaldi veneziano europeo*, ed. Francesco Degrada (Florence, 1980), pp. 67–75

Vickers, Brian: *Shakespeare: The Critical Heritage, V, 1765–1774* (London, 1979)

Walsh, Marcus: *Shakespeare, Milton, and Eighteenth-Century Literary Editing* (Cambridge, 1997)

IMAGE CREDITS

© Aidan McRae Thomson: 25, 71 (above)

Used by kind permission of the Master and Fellows of Balliol College Oxford: 7

Reproduced with the permission of Birmingham Libraries & Archives: 14 (Norton 1504) (right)

By permission of Bloomsbury Publishers Plc: 10 (right)

© The British Library Board: 10 (80.i.23.(2.)) (left), 11 (11824.g.1.), 18 (468.b.1.) (above), 24 (604.e.20.(4.)), 41 (R.M. 7.g.22.), 68 (R.M. 20.g.3. folio 99v)

The Brotherton Collection, Leeds University Library: 45

Reproduced by kind permission of the Syndics of Cambridge University Library: 14 (I.16.30 (F)) (left), 16 (Syn.1.79.6), 18 (Ff.11.31) (below), 28 (Syn.1.79.6) (below)

City of London, London Metropolitan Archives: 6, 17

Lady Charlotte Dinan: back cover, 32-3 (above)

Gerald Coke Handel Foundation: 9 (acc.no. 6537), 23 (acc.no. 2378) (below), 28 (acc.no. 7701) (above), 29 (acc.no. 1730), 44 (acc.no. 7603), 54-5 (acc.no. 1730), 56 (acc.no. 1286), 57 (acc.no. 7691), 60 (acc.no. 7692), 61 (acc.no. 6978), 64-5 (acc.no. 1827), 69 (acc.no. 1730)

Hampshire Records Office: 46 (9M73/G57), 50 (9M73/G500/2)

Handel & Haydn Society, Boston: 59

© Handel House Museum Trust Ltd.: front cover (1997.28), ii (1997.28), 20 (1998.128(1))

From the Newman Flower collection at The Henry Watson Music Library, with kind permission of Manchester Libraries, Information and Archives, Manchester City Council: 42

Reproduced by courtesy of the University Librarian and Director, The John Rylands Library, The University of Manchester: 8

Leicester Arts and Museum Service: 12, 71 (below)

With acknowledgement to the Leicestershire, Leicester & Rutland Record Office: 5 (below)

Image provided courtesy of the Library of Congress, Performing Arts reading room: 43

© National Portrait Gallery, London: vi (NPG 6724), 22 (D3231), 48 (NPG 3970)

Paul Sacher Collection, Paul Sacher Foundation (Basel, Switzerland): 23 (above)

Private lenders: 2, 4 (below), 4-5 (above), 15, 26, 27, 30, 40

RIBA Library Drawings and Archives Collections: 19, 33 (below), 34, 35 (all)

Sheffield Galleries and Museums Trust, UK / Photo © Museums Sheffield / The Bridgeman Art Library: 36

© Victoria and Albert Museum, London: 39

INDEX